HOT, HOTTER, HOTTEST

HOT, HOTTER, HOTTEST

50 Fiery Recipes from around the World

Janet Hazen

Photographs by Joyce Oudkerk Pool
Food Styling by Sue White

CHRONICLE BOOKS

SAN FRANCISCO

Library of Congress Cataloging in Publication Data.
Hazen, Janet.
    Hot, hotter, hottest : 50 fiery recipes /
by Janet Hazen ; photographs by Joyce Oudkerk Pool ;
food styling by Sue White.
        p.   cm.
    Includes index.
    ISBN 0-8118-0079-2 (pbk.)
    1. Cookery, International. 2. Spices. 3. Condiments.
    I. Title.
TX725.A1H354   1992   91-30630
641.59—dc20   CIP

Printed in Hong Kong.

Composition: Ann Flanagan Typography
Book Design: Brenda Rae Eno
Calligraphy: Georgia Deaver

Distributed in Canada by Raincoast Books,
112 East Third Avenue, Vancouver, B.C. V5T 1C8

10   9   8   7   6   5   4

Chronicle Books
275 Fifth Street
San Francisco, CA 94103

CONTENTS

LIST OF RECIPES

Sauces and Condiments

Desserts

Beverages

IT WASN'T SO LONG AGO THAT PEOPLE ACTUALLY HAD TO BE *warned* about hot spicy food. Some had to be coaxed to sample just a morsel of the wicked stuff. Well, the tables have taken a turn. Droves of hungry "hotheads" now flood grocery stores, restaurants, cafés, and farmers' markets. They are in search of foods that will bring tears to the eyes, lightning bolts to the sinuses, a tingle to the lips, sweat to the brow, and heat that surges through the body. As those who crave these sensations know, once a hothead, always a hothead. North Americans have only recently discovered the myriad sources of "heat," but now the United States, in its love affair with incendiary ingredients, is pushing the frontiers.

Indian, Mexican, and Thai cuisines are what come to mind when most people think of hot food. Upon closer examination, however, it is apparent that almost every major cuisine has some sort of heat. Certainly Asian, Latin, and African peoples incorporate many torrid ingredients in their diets, but even the northern European countries and North America include hot mustards, black pepper, or horseradish in some traditional dishes. Peppercorns, chilies, mustard, and ginger were originally used to mask the rancid flavor in certain foods in hot, humid climates, and they are still used in many countries medicinally. Red and green chili peppers are thought of as primary components in most hot dishes, but the world of heat is not limited to fresh chilies, nor does it end with those that are dried, smoked, or pickled. Black, white, pink, and green peppercorns appear on many pantry shelves; their warm flavors and heating qualities are treasured by those who love spicy food. Certainly pink peppercorns aren't hot, but when combined with white or black peppercorns, they lend a warm and inviting flavor sensation.

Dried mustard powders and prepared mustards from around the world are also standard fare in most kitchens, and for good reason, since it is mustard that adds depth and zing to many favorite dishes. Mustard eaten alone can be painfully hot, but once it is cooked it mellows and loses much of its sting. The same goes for horseradish, but since we usually use it in raw form, most folks do associate this pungent root with its distinctive sinus-clearing abilities.

Fresh ginger, often reserved for some singular Asian dish, offers a refreshing form of heat and spice. Raw ginger is enticing and invigorating, but in this form it is too pungent and too hot for many to eat. As with horseradish and mustard, ginger's heat can be softened with cooking. Hotheads naturally prefer mustard, horseradish, and ginger in their most robust and pure forms (and may use an abundance of black pepper at the table when at a loss for anything else that's spicy), but even the more subtle uses of these ingredients add pleasant zing and heat to most any dish.

The first time I sampled a jalapeño pepper I had the entire restaurant staff waiting on me at one time. Well, they weren't exactly *waiting* on me, they were administering first aid to my scorched mouth and lips. My companion, with his asbestos mouth, not only was accustomed to eating raw chili peppers but was virtually addicted to the things. This was my first lesson in heat tolerance. The moral of the story: just because the guy next to you can eat a hot food, doesn't mean you can. Everyone has a different level of tolerance, and what is unbearably hot to one is mild and even bland to another. For this reason it wasn't easy to classify the level of heat in each dish. The ratings given are from 1 to 10, with 10 the hottest. Only a few recipes in the book generate the very highest level of heat, and naturally they are all in the chili chapter. Mind you, there are plenty of incendiary dishes in the other chapters, as well as some very mild ones. The most subtle heat is generated by recipes for mustard and horseradish, since once their vital oils are heated much of the heat dissipates. (Even the most dedicated hothead will appreciate a full-bodied, just-spicy meal now and then.) For the record, my painful jalapeño lesson occurred more than seventeen years ago, and since that time I have been at the head of the line for raw and cooked chilies and ginger, potent mustards, fiery horseradish sauces, and dishes bursting with pepper.

Worth considering along with the sheer fun of eating hot foods is their healthfulness. Oftentimes a dish that is highly seasoned requires no salt, or very little. Since most of us try to avoid excess sodium in our diets, adding spicy or hot ingredients becomes not only a tasty alternative but a sensible and healthful one as well. Moreover, the five main sources of heat in this book offer many health rewards in their own right. You can be confident that these recipes will leave you feeling satiated, happy, healthy, and even well traveled.

GINGER

In THE 1800S, BANANA BOATS FROM THE CARIBBEAN LOADED WITH mangoes, papayas, pineapples, and guavas for the Southern cities of the United States would occasionally hold a few treasured crates of fresh ginger. These exotic "roots" began to appear in sweet and savory dishes, but the rest of the country still knew ginger as an innocuous powdered substance sold in small tins. (Ginger is actually not a root but a rhizome, or underground stem; it can produce shoots, something a root can't do.) It grows in hot, tropical climates, so it is used primarily in the cooking of Asia, the Mediterranean, the Middle East, Africa, and the Caribbean. It really wasn't until the Vietnam War and the increased travel to Asia that most of the United States discovered fresh ginger. And now, with the great influx of southeast Asian immigrants throughout the country, fresh ginger is as common as fresh garlic.

Native to the East Indies, Malaysia, and New Guinea, ginger was cultivated by the Chinese as early as the sixth century B.C. Arab traders probably brought it to the Mediterranean some time before the first century A.D. Long known for its medicinal qualities, ginger has a reputation for stimulating circulation, clearing bronchial congestion, combating colds and flu, cleansing kidneys, alleviating flatulence, curing skin infections and upset stomachs, and soothing painful joints, as well as being an aphrodisiac.

The exterior of ginger root is light tan, and the interior flesh has a pale, greenish yellow color. Fresh ginger has a thin skin and the flesh is at once fibrous and juicy. Choose roots that are hard and fairly smooth in texture, and free of green shoots. Young ginger is often sold in Asian markets and is softer, a bit milder, and has a thinner skin. It does not need to be peeled, but mature ginger, the more common of the two, needs to be peeled before it is used in most recipes. Peel the skin with a sharp paring knife, removing the protruding roots and nubs as you go. When ginger is kept too long it becomes dry and fibrous, but it still can be used in an emergency. When peeling older ginger, remove more of the skin so that the juicier, more flavorful flesh is revealed. Ginger has a bright, clean, sparkling aroma, and is peppery and pungent when eaten uncooked. Store fresh ginger in a cool, dry place for up to two months. It keeps best at cool room temperature, but in very hot, humid climates you may wrap it in plastic and store it in the refrigerator for up to one month.

Enhancing both sweet and savory dishes, ginger can be bitingly hot and pungent, moderately spicy and warm, or subtle and barely noticeable. Those effects are determined by how much ginger is used, and, as with garlic, how finely it is cut and how long it is cooked. Ginger is generally peeled and sliced into thin rounds, cut into thin julienne shapes, diced, chopped, minced, or grated. Because the root is so fibrous, care must be taken to remove the "hairs" or fibers that are separated out in grated or shredded ginger. Fresh ginger is also made into pickled ginger, which is usually served with Japanese sushi and sashimi; and crystallized ginger, which is used in baking and sweet dishes. The root is also preserved and stored in attractive jars. Dried, it is ground and sold in jars or cans.

To cut ginger into slivers: Peel the root and cut at an angle to produce oval shapes about 1/8-inch thick. Lay the flat oval shapes on the cutting board so that they barely overlap. Cutting the long way on the oval, slice into very thin, long pieces.

To dice ginger: Peel the root and slice one very thin piece from one side. Lay the root flat on the cutting board on this flat, cut side. Slice the root lengthwise; 1/4-inch wide for small dice, 1/2-inch for medium, and 3/4-inch for large. Stack the slices of ginger and cut again lengthwise into the appropriate-size strips. Make the final cuts by slicing across into the appropriate-size dice.

To grate ginger: Peel the root and grate on a metal grater. Use the finest setting if you want pulp and juice, medium for some pulp and a little juice, and a jumbo setting for small bits of the root.

Ginger roots can be as thick as a silver dollar and as narrow as a nickel, but most roots are about the thickness of a quarter. The recipes following specify amounts in length measurements, and since this isn't exact, I also give here a standard cup measure for an average-size ginger root's yield when finely chopped. You really don't have to use an exact measurement of ginger, or of most other ingredients for that matter, but some cooks feel better with a little more control over the recipe.

2-inch piece ginger root = about 3 tablespoons
4-inch piece ginger root = about 1/2 cup
6-inch piece ginger root = about 2/3 cup
8-inch piece ginger root = about 1 cup

Spicy Ginger Syrup

2 pounds ginger root, sliced
into ½-inch pieces

1 stick cinnamon

7 quarts cold water

6 cups sugar

When I was traveling in Southeast Asia, I spent many an afternoon sipping icy ginger drinks made from what tasted like pure ginger and carbonated water. Upon returning home, I decided to make my own ginger syrup. With this sweet but hot syrup you can make your own ginger ale and brighten desserts, or use it to flavor vodka and sweeten tea and in sauces, marinades, and meat or poultry glazes.
Makes about 3 cups. Hot: rated 2

Place the ginger, cinnamon, and 4 quarts of the water in an 8- or 10-quart heavy-bottomed pan. Bring to a boil over high heat. Boil for 45 minutes, stirring occasionally. Add the remaining water and boil for 45 minutes. Cool slightly, strain, and return the liquid to the pan.

Add the sugar to the liquid, bring to a boil, and cook over high heat for 20 to 30 minutes, or until the liquid is thick and syrupy. (Do not leave the pot unattended, as the syrup tends to boil over.) Remove from the heat and cool to room temperature before storing in a tightly sealed glass container. Store in the refrigerator for up to 3 months.

To use Spicy Ginger Syrup: Add 2 tablespoons to a glass of tonic or sparkling water, and ice, and mix well. For desserts: Drizzle syrup over poached or fresh fruit or over sliced cake, or use it as a glaze for tarts.

Sizzling Prawns with Ginger

This Chinese-style stir-fry dish is easy to prepare. You may increase the Chinese hot chili paste to suit your taste, but I suggest you sample the paste before you add it to the entire dish—some commercial chili pastes are extremely hot, while others are quite tame in comparison. Serve this colorful, light dinner or lunch dish with steamed rice, fried noodles, or on a bed of mixed greens for a cross-cultural meal.

Makes 4 to 6 servings.   *Hottest: rated 8*

3 tablespoons peanut oil

1 pound medium-sized prawns, peeled and tails removed

1 large red bell pepper, cut in julienne

4-inch piece ginger root, peeled and finely chopped

4 cloves garlic, thinly sliced

1 teaspoon Chinese hot chili paste

2 tablespoons dry sherry

1 small bunch green onions, trimmed, cut in 1-inch pieces

¼ cup soy sauce

¾ cup toasted peanuts

¾ cup chopped cilantro

Heat a very large nonstick sauté pan or a large wok over high heat until it is hot. Add the oil and heat until it just begins to smoke. Add the prawns, red bell pepper, ginger, garlic, chili paste, and sherry, and cook over high heat for 1 minute, stirring all the while. Add the onions, soy sauce, and peanuts and cook for 1 minute, stirring constantly. Add half of the cilantro and mix well.

Turn the prawns onto a large platter, garnish with the remaining cilantro, and serve immediately with steamed rice or noodles.

Warm Thai Ginger Beef Salad

1 pound filet mignon steaks, trimmed of fat

4 cloves garlic, thinly sliced

4-inch piece ginger root, peeled and minced

2 tablespoons *nuoc cham* (fish sauce)

2 tablespoons soy sauce

1 tablespoon sugar

Dressing:

½ cup peanut oil

¼ cup fresh lime juice

1 small red onion, halved and thinly sliced

3 cloves garlic, minced

3-inch piece ginger root, peeled and slivered

1 to 2 red or green jalapeño peppers, stemmed, cut in thin rounds

Salt and pepper, to taste

1 small head butter lettuce, leaves separated

½ cup chopped cilantro, for garnish

½ cup mint leaves, for garnish

This classic Thai beef salad is served barely warm, and is delicious for lunch or a light supper with fried noodles or steamed rice. Icy cold Thai beer would be a good accompaniment to this spicy, flavorful Southeast Asian dish.
Makes 4 servings.   *Hotter: rated 6*

Place the steaks in a nonreactive bowl with the garlic, ginger, *nuoc cham*, and soy sauce, and the sugar; mix well and let stand at room temperature for 30 minutes to 1 hour.

To make the dressing: Place 6 tablespoons of the peanut oil in a small bowl. Using a wire whisk, incorporate the lime juice a little at a time, whisking all the while to form a smooth emulsion. Add the onion, garlic, ginger, and jalapeño pepper; mix well. Season with salt and pepper and set aside until needed.

Heat the remaining 2 tablespoons of peanut oil in a wok or a large nonstick sauté pan over high heat. When the oil is hot, add the steaks along with some of the bits of ginger and garlic, and cook over moderately high heat for 2 to 3 minutes per side. Remove from the pan and cool slightly.

Cut the steaks into ¼-inch thick slices and add to the dressing. Mix well and arrange the dressed beef on beds of butter lettuce. Garnish with the cilantro and mint, and serve immediately.

Ginger Squash Soup

2 pounds winter squash
(Hubbard, acorn, butternut,
or pumpkin)

1 onion, cut in medium dice

2 cloves garlic, minced

1 tablespoon ground coriander
seed

1 teaspoon ground allspice

3 tablespoons olive oil

4 tablespoons (½ stick)
unsalted butter

6-inch piece ginger root,
peeled and coarsely chopped

1½ quarts light chicken stock

Salt and pepper, to taste

¾ cup crème fraîche (or sour
cream thinned with water),
for garnish

Pansies or other edible flowers,
for garnish (optional)

Aromatic and pleasantly sweet, this gold-colored winter squash soup makes a heartwarming fall or winter lunch. Serve with country-style bread and a green salad.
Makes 6 servings.

Hot: rated 2

Preheat oven to 425°F.

Cut the squash in half lengthwise, seed it, and place cut side down in a shallow baking dish. Add water to a depth of 2 inches. Bake for 25 to 30 minutes or until the squash is tender. Remove from the oven and cool to room temperature. When cool enough to handle, remove the pulp from the skin and place in a bowl. Set aside until needed.

In a very large pot, cook the onion, garlic, and spices in the olive oil and butter over moderate heat for 15 minutes, stirring frequently. Add the ginger, reserved squash, and chicken stock and bring to a boil over high heat. Cook for 5 minutes, stirring constantly. Remove from the heat and cool to room temperature.

Purée the soup in batches, using a blender. Strain through a fine wire mesh and return to the saucepan. Bring to a boil over high heat; cook for 10 minutes, and season with salt and pepper. Drizzle crème fraîche, float pansies (if using them), and serve hot.

Tuna Tartare with Ginger

Ruby red and jewel-like, a Japanese-style tuna dish makes a stunning appetizer, but it is also good served with sautéed vegetables for a light supper in hot weather. Be sure to get fresh tuna from your fishmonger, as it is eaten uncooked, sushi style. Makes 4 to 6 servings. Hot: rated 3

Using a very sharp cleaver or knife, mince the tuna by hand, rather than in a food processor. (The texture of very fresh fish is important to the dish's appeal, and cutting with a knife by hand is the best way to achieve the desired texture.) Place the tuna in a glass or plastic bowl.

Add the sesame oil, sherry, vinegar, chives, and ginger; mix well. Taste and season with salt and black pepper if needed. Refrigerate until ready to serve, but is best eaten right away. Arrange on a bed of greens and garnish with the sesame seeds and optionally, chive blossoms.

1½ pounds lean, fresh tuna fillet

2 tablespoons Asian sesame oil

2 tablespoons dry sherry or mirin (sweet rice wine)

1 tablespoon seasoned rice wine vinegar

½ cup minced chives

4-inch piece ginger root, peeled and slivered

Salt and pepper, to taste

Mixed greens: baby mustard greens, or rocket, mizuna, or baby lettuces

¼ cup black sesame seeds, for garnish

Chive blossoms, for garnish (optional)

Hunan Scallops with Black Beans and Ginger-Chili Oil

Ginger-Chili Oil:

½ cup peanut oil

4 dried red chilies, crushed

4-inch piece ginger root, peeled and minced

2 cloves garlic, thinly sliced

2 tablespoons Asian sesame oil

2 tablespoons soy sauce

2 tablespoons peanut oil

4-inch piece ginger root, peeled and slivered

1 pound scallops, muscles removed

3 tablespoons preserved black beans

3 tablespoons dry sherry

1 large red bell pepper, cut in julienne

2 cups fresh spinach leaves

Hunan-style Chinese cuisine is characterized in part by the abundance of ginger, garlic, and hot chilies. This fiery seafood dish is beautiful served on a bed of spinach or shredded green cabbage, or served with steamed rice for a more traditional meal.
Makes 4 servings.   *Hotter: rated 6*

To make the Ginger-Chili Oil: In a heavy-bottomed skillet, heat the peanut oil, chilies, ginger, and garlic over moderate heat, stirring constantly for 2 minutes, until it begins to sizzle. Add the sesame oil and soy sauce and cook for 2 minutes. Remove from the heat and cool slightly. Strain through a fine wire mesh and set aside until needed.

A scant 5 minutes before you want to serve the scallops, heat the peanut oil in a wok or very large nonstick sauté pan over high heat. When the oil is very hot, add the ginger and scallops. Cook for 2 minutes, stirring all the while. Add the black beans, sherry, and red bell pepper, and cook for 1 more minute, stirring constantly. Remove from the heat and arrange on top of the spinach leaves. Drizzle with the Ginger-Chili Oil and serve immediately.

Grilled Ginger-Orange Chicken with Ginger Sauce

Marinade:

1½ cups peanut oil

½ cup orange juice

¼ cup soy sauce

¾ cup honey

12-inch piece ginger root, peeled and minced

⅓ cup ground ginger powder

2 tablespoons ground coriander

1 large chicken plus 2 legs (about 4 pounds), cut into serving pieces

Sauce:

½ cup corn syrup

3 tablespoons rice wine vinegar

3 tablespoons fresh lime juice

2 cloves garlic, finely chopped

4-inch piece ginger root, peeled and finely chopped

Salt and pepper, to taste

Cilantro sprigs, for garnish

Most all Asian-style marinades are wonderful with chicken or turkey, as they are aromatic and flavorful but don't overpower the delicate flavors of the meat. Basmati rice or noodles served along with a green vegetable would make this a complete and simple dinner.
Makes 4 to 6 servings.   *Hot: rated 3*

To make the marinade: Place the olive oil in a bowl. Slowly add the orange juice, whisking all the while to make a smooth emulsion. Slowly add the soy sauce and honey, whisking all the while. Add the ginger and coriander; mix well.

Arrange the chicken in a shallow nonreactive vessel and pour the marinade over it. You may use a plastic bag for this (be sure to leave it in a container in case the bag leaks). Marinate for 1 to 2 days in the refrigerator, rotating the chicken so that the marinade comes in contact with the meat at all times.

To make the sauce: Combine all the ingredients except the cilantro in a nonreactive bowl; mix well and season with salt and pepper.

Prepare a charcoal grill. When the coals are medium hot (a light layer of gray ash will cover the coals), place the chicken on the grill skin side down. Cook the chicken, rotating it to prevent it from burning, for 35 to 40 minutes, or until it is dark brown and the meat is cooked all the way to the bone. The cooking time will vary according to the heat of your fire. Remove the chicken and let stand at room temperature for 5 minutes before serving. Garnish with cilantro and serve with the sauce.

Spiced Indian Cauliflower with Ginger

If you would like to make this a true vegetarian dish, omit the chicken stock and use a light tomato or vegetable broth instead. This spicy Indian vegetable dish is excellent with lamb, chicken, or beef dishes, and also goes well with stewed lentils and Indian breads.
Makes 4 to 6 servings.   Hotter: rated 6

Place the ginger, garlic, spices, olive oil, and ½ cup of the chicken stock in a blender. Purée until fairly smooth. Remove from the blender.

Heat a deep-sided, nonstick skillet large enough to accommodate all the cauliflower. Over high heat, cook the ginger paste and cauliflower, stirring constantly, for 1 minute. Add the remaining chicken stock and bring to a boil still over high heat.

Reduce the heat to moderate and cook, uncovered, until the cauliflower is almost tender—7 to 8 minutes, or until almost all the liquid has evaporated. Add the lemon juice, red pepper, and cilantro and cook for 3 to 4 minutes. Season with salt and pepper, mix well, and serve immediately.

4-inch piece ginger root, peeled and coarsely chopped

3 cloves garlic

1 tablespoon ground coriander

1 teaspoon each ground turmeric, mace, cayenne, and cumin

¼ cup olive oil

2 cups chicken stock

8 cups or 3 small heads cauliflower, cut in 1-inch flowerettes

Juice from 2 lemons

1 large red bell pepper, cut in small dice

1 cup chopped cilantro

Salt and pepper, to taste

Eggplant Ravioli with Ginger-Cilantro Sauce

A blend of Italian and Asian ingredients and cooking methods make this a whimsical cross-cultural dish. Mediterranean herbs, eggplant, vinegar, and nuts form a robust filling, but the delicate Asian wonton wrappers and barely thickened sauce lend a refined texture and elegance to these raviolis.
Makes 4 to 6 servings (24 raviolis)   *Hotter: rated 4*

Sauce:

1 quart chicken stock

4-inch piece ginger root, peeled and slivered

2 tablespoons cornstarch

½ cup dry sherry

1 teaspoon dried red pepper flakes

1 cup chopped cilantro

Filling:

1 large onion, cut in small dice

3 cloves garlic, minced

2 teaspoons each dried rosemary and thyme and ground coriander

⅓ cup olive oil

6-inch piece ginger root, peeled and minced

3 medium Japanese or Italian eggplants, cut in small dice

¼ cup balsamic vinegar

½ cup toasted pine nuts

3 tablespoons tomato paste

Salt and pepper, to taste

To make the sauce: Place the chicken stock and ginger in a large pan. Bring to a boil over high heat. Cook over high heat for 5 minutes. Combine the cornstarch and sherry in a small bowl; mix well. Slowly add this "slurry" to the chicken stock, stirring as you go. Continue boiling until the mixture starts to thicken. Reduce the heat and cook for 10 minutes over moderate heat. (You will add the red pepper flakes and cilantro just before serving.)

To make the filling: Cook the onion, garlic, and herbs in the olive oil over moderate heat for 15 minutes, stirring from time to time. Add the ginger and eggplant and cook over high heat for 5 minutes, stirring constantly. Add the vinegar and cook over moderate heat for 5 to 7 minutes, stirring frequently, until the eggplant is soft and tender. Add the pine nuts and tomato paste, mix well, and season with salt and pepper. Cool to room temperature.

To make the raviolis: Combine the cornstarch with the water in a small bowl. Arrange 10 skins on a flat surface. Lightly brush each skin with the slurry. Place 1½ to 2 teaspoons of filling in the center of each skin. Cover with a second skin, pressing the two sides together from the filling out to the edge of the skin, removing any air bubbles as you secure the two skins. Place on a sheet pan and continue making the raviolis until all the filling is used up. Refrigerate for up to 1 hour before cooking.

The skins become a bit soggy if they are stored in the refrigerator for longer than one hour. If you can't cook the raviolis within that time, freeze them on a sheet pan. When they are completely frozen, place the raviolis in a bag and store in the freezer until you are ready to cook.

1 package potsticker or gyoza skins (about 60 skins)

¼ cup cornstarch

1 cup water

To cook the raviolis: Bring a large pot of salted water to boil over high heat. When the water is boiling, add a batch and cook for 3 to 4 minutes (6 to 7 minutes if frozen), or until they are tender and the skins are transparent all the way through. Remove with a slotted spoon and drain in a colander. (The raviolis will stick together if you let them sit in the colander for more than a couple of minutes. If this happens, place the clump in a bowl of warm water and carefully separate with your fingers.)

Immediately place the raviolis in shallow bowls. Add some of the red pepper flakes and cilantro to each bowl and drizzle with some of the sauce.

Poached Nectarines with Ginger and Crème Fraîche

2 cups water

2 cups fruity white wine

2 cups sugar

4-inch piece ginger root, peeled and thinly sliced

6 ripe but firm nectarines, quartered and pits removed

1 teaspoon almond extract

1 cup crème fraîche (or sour cream thinned with a little water)

¼ cup candied ginger, slivered

Mint sprigs, for garnish

Spicy yet refreshing, this fruit concoction is a wonderful warm-weather dessert. Use apricots, peaches, or even peeled oranges in combination with the nectarines if you like. When the ginger cooks in the sweet liquid the slices curl in a most delightful way, and add texture and intriguing shapes to this fruit dessert.
Makes 4 to 6 servings   *Hot: rated 3*

Place the water, wine, sugar, and ginger in a heavy-bottomed saucepan. Bring to a boil over high heat and cook for 20 minutes, stirring frequently. Add the nectarines, reduce the heat to moderately low, and cook until the fruit is tender but not mushy, 2 to 3 minutes. Remove from the heat and add the almond extract.

Serve warm or at room temperature in a little of the cooking liquid and a drizzle of crème fraîche, topped with a few slivers of candied ginger and sprigs of mint.

HORSERADISH COMES FROM THE ROOT OF A PLANT IN THE CABBAGE family native to southeastern Europe. It has been used for both culinary and medicinal purposes for centuries; the Egyptians knew about horseradish as long ago as 1500 B.C., and the spicy root is said to have been one of the five bitter herbs that Jews ate during Passover. Early Greeks used it medicinally as well as an aphrodisiac. Greek legend has it that the radish is worth its weight in lead, the beet its weight in silver, the horseradish its weight in gold.

By the late Middle Ages, horseradish was growing wild in northern Europe and Britain, where it was thought to cure gout and rheumatism. By the sixteenth century, it had gained popularity in Scandinavia and Germany, but it wasn't really accepted in Britain as a flavoring ingredient until the seventeenth century. Mustard had been the favored condiment in Britain until this time. When horseradish eventually took mustard's place, it was served in a side dish with roast beef, pickled fish, and strong-tasting, cooked oily fish such as herring and mackerel. Germans called it *meerrettich* (sea radish), because it grew near the sea; the English mispronunciation "mareradish" is believed to have led to its current name.

Early settlers brought horseradish to North America in the early 1800s. (It soon grew wild here, too.) Commercial cultivation in the United States began around 1850, and the current annual production of prepared horseradish is approximately six million gallons.

Prepared horseradish in jars is available in all grocery stores, and it can be kept in the refrigerator for up to six months after opening. Keep in mind that prepared horseradish loses its pungency over time, even when refrigerated. Also, it contains some combination of vinegar, spices, oil, and seasonings, and its texture will make the foods that you add it to creamier and softer than the fresh form will. But when a recipe calls for fresh horseradish root and you can't find it, the commercial prepared variety is a fair substitute.

Most of the recipes here call for fresh horseradish. Purchase roots that are hard, dry, and as free from knots and dents as possible. Store in a cool, dry place for up to two months, or wrapped in plastic in the refrigerator for several months. If you do not find horseradish in fresh root form, ask your produce person to order some for you. Many restaurants and catering companies use the root, so it is available.

The long, slender fresh root is extremely biting in its raw form but loses some if its zing when cooked, or when combined with vinegar. Most horseradish roots are about a foot long and the size of a half-dollar in circumference. One end is knobby and bulbous, but 90 percent of the root is usually of the same width, forming a long, regular cylinder shape. Tiny fibers or hairs cover areas of the surface, though for the most part the root is fairly smooth and even in texture. Caked-on dirt usually masks the pale yellow exterior of the horseradish; once cleaned, the root resembles a parsnip in color.

The thin outer skin must be peeled before using the root; you can do this with a paring knife. Once peeled, the root is creamy white and fairly aromatic. Your eyes won't start to water until you chop or grate the root, and when you do, be prepared with a handkerchief! The root may be sliced, chopped, grated, or shredded by hand or machine, but by any method the strong oils will permeate the air and send tears streaming down your cheeks. Horseradish is commonly combined with creamy, bland substances such as heavy cream, sour cream, butter, cultured cream, or cream cheese, to make sharp but pleasing sauces or dips. Since the root does lose pungency when cooked, a slow-cooking dish that contains horseradish will have only a hint of the flavor and very little heat, whereas a dish that contains barely cooked or raw horseradish will be invigorating and very hot. Japanese horseradish, an entirely different species, produces a green-colored powder called wasabi. It is used in soups, sauces, and in the preparation of sushi and sashimi. Both types of root can clear the nasal passages within seconds. This characteristic, along with an unmistakable flavor, sets horseradish apart from all other condiments and flavoring ingredients.

To grate horseradish, as called for in recipes that follow, use the finest setting of the grater. Since every root is a different size, it is impossible to give exact inch measurements for recipes. As with ginger root, precision is not critical.

**1-inch piece fresh horseradish root =
about ¼ cup grated
2-inch piece horseradish =
about ½ cup grated
4- to 5-inch piece horseradish =
about 1 cup grated**

Classic Shrimp Cocktail

1 cup catsup or cocktail sauce

2- to 3-inch piece horseradish root, peeled and grated

1 clove garlic, minced

3 tablespoons fresh lemon juice

½ teaspoon celery seed

Dash Tabasco sauce

Salt and pepper, to taste

1 pound large prawns

3 tablespoons minced parsley, for garnish

There isn't much to improve on when it comes to this classic American appetizer. Fresh horseradish, rather than prepared, adds depth and more zing to this already pungent red sauce. You can serve the seafood on a bed of shredded cabbage, greens, or in the traditional shrimp cocktail glass. An ice cold beer is the perfect beverage with this dish.
Makes 4 servings.   *Hottest: rated 8*

In a nonreactive bowl, combine the catsup, horseradish, garlic, lemon juice, celery seed, Tabasco sauce, and salt and pepper; mix well. This will keep in the refrigerator for up to 2 weeks.

Bring a large pot of water to boil over high heat. When the water is boiling, add the prawns and stir. Cook for 1 to 1½ minutes, or until the prawns are brightly colored and cooked through. Do not overcook the prawns. Drain and rinse with cold water.

When the prawns are cool enough to handle, remove the shells and tails. Combine with the cocktail sauce and refrigerate for 1 hour, or arrange the prawns around a bowl of the sauce. Serve chilled, with chopped parsley for a garnish.

Twice-Baked Potatoes with Horseradish Cream

Rich, filling, and satisfying, these baked potatoes with a cheesy horseradish filling are great with grilled meats or chicken, or served with sausages for a hearty breakfast.
Makes 5 or 10 servings.   Hotter: rated 6

5 very large baking potatoes, scrubbed clean

1 pound sliced bacon

1 large onion, cut in small dice

1 teaspoon fennel seed

½ teaspoon celery seed

1 bunch green onions, trimmed and finely chopped

½ pound sharp cheddar cheese, grated

1 cup sour cream

6-inch piece horseradish root, peeled and grated

Salt and pepper, to taste

½ cup minced parsley, for garnish

Preheat oven to 400° F.

Bake the potatoes on the middle rack of the oven until tender when pierced with a fork, about 1 hour and 10 minutes. Remove from the oven and slice in half, lengthwise. Using a spoon, carefully scoop out the potato pulp, taking care not to break the skin. Place pulp in a bowl.

Meanwhile, cook the bacon until crisp. Remove with a slotted spoon and drain on paper towels. Finely chop and add to the potato pulp. Cook the diced onion and spices in the remaining bacon fat over moderately high heat for 10 minutes, stirring frequently. Add the green onions and cook for 1 minute. Remove with a slotted spoon and add to the potato-bacon mixture along with the cheddar cheese, sour cream, and horseradish. Mix well and season with salt and pepper.

Divide the mixture among the potato shells, mounding the filling. Bake filled potatoes in a lightly greased baking pan for 25 to 30 minutes, or until the filling is hot. Garnish with minced parsley and serve immediately.

Grilled Mackerel with Horseradish

Pleasantly oily mackerel is a natural companion to the piquant flavors of horse-radish. Sauced with only a few assertive ingredients and grilled over hot coals, this dish allows the true flavors of both the fish and the horseradish to come through with clarity and depth.
Makes 4 servings.   *Hotter: rated 4*

4   1-pound mackerels, head on and cleaned

¾ cup olive oil

Black pepper

2 cups parsley sprigs

4-inch piece fresh horseradish root, peeled and finely chopped

1 teaspoon each dried red pepper flakes and rosemary

⅓ cup fresh lemon juice

Rosemary and thyme sprigs, for garnish

Coat the fish with some of the olive oil, and dust with black pepper. Prepare a charcoal grill. When the coals are medium hot (the coals will have a thin layer of gray ash), place the fish on the grill and cook for 7 to 8 minutes. Carefully flip the fish over and cook the second side for 6 to 7 minutes, or until the fish is opaque all the way through. Remove from the grill and arrange on a bed of the parsley on a large platter.

Heat the remaining oil, the horseradish, the red pepper flakes and rosemary, and the lemon juice in a small saucepan over moderate heat. Cook for 1 to 2 minutes, or until the bits of horseradish begin to sizzle. Remove from the heat and drizzle over the fish. Garnish with the rosemary and thyme sprigs and serve immediately.

German Horseradish Sauce

This German sauce is quite mild. It is very good with wild game and poultry, though it is traditionally served with boiled meats or sausage. For a more assertive flavor, add an extra ¼ cup of uncooked, grated horseradish just before serving.
Makes about 1¼ cups.   *Hot: rated 2*

5- to 6-inch piece horseradish root, peeled and grated

½ teaspoon dried thyme

4 tablespoons (½ stick) unsalted butter

1¼ cups unsalted beef broth or stock

¼ cup fine dry bread crumbs

⅓ cup dry sherry

Salt and pepper, to taste

Place 1 cup of the horseradish and the thyme and butter in a saucepan. Cook over moderate heat for 2 to 3 minutes, stirring all the while. Add the beef broth and bread crumbs and bring to a boil over high heat, stirring constantly. Reduce the heat to moderate and cook for 10 minutes. Add the sherry and remaining horseradish and cook 2 minutes. Season with salt and pepper and serve warm.

Horseradish-Crusted Salmon

2 eggs, lightly beaten

½ cup whole milk

8-inch piece horseradish root, peeled and grated

1 teaspoon salt

4 8-ounce salmon fillets

¼ cup light olive oil

The first time I had horseradish paired with salmon I thought it would over-whelm the delicate, sweet flavor of the fish, but the combination was really excit-ing and quite successful. The crust adds flavor and helps to seal in the juices of the fish. A drizzle of crème fraîche or thinned sour cream is a pleasing garnish for this savory fish fillet.

Makes 4 servings.　　　　　　　　　　　　　　　　　　　　Hot: rated 2

In a shallow baking dish large enough to accommodate all the fillets, combine the eggs, milk, horseradish root, and salt; mix well. Pat the salmon dry with paper towels. Coat each piece of salmon with the horseradish batter, taking care to press the horseradish onto all sides of the fish.

Heat the olive oil in a nonstick sauté pan large enough to accommodate all the fish. When the oil is hot, but not smoking, add the fish and cook over moderately high heat for 3 to 4 minutes on the first side. Carefully flip the fish over and cook the second side for 3 to 4 minutes. Do not overcook the fish or it will be dry and tasteless. Remove from the pan and serve immediately.

Lamb and Horseradish Tartlettes

The savory filling for these individual tartlettes is best if made 1 or 2 days in advance. The dough can also be made a couple of days ahead, so this would be an ideal appetizer or light lunch for company. A salad of sweet and bitter greens or a green bean salad would go nicely with these little pies. Serve with prepared horseradish if you prefer a more pronounced flavor.
Makes 6 4-inch tartlettes.   Hot: rated 1

To make the dough: Place the flour and salt in a medium-sized bowl; mix well. Add the shortening and butter and, using your hands, mix lightly and quickly until the mixture resembles coarse meal. Add enough water to make the dough come together and form a ball. Wrap in plastic and refrigerate for 2 hours or up to 2 days.

Preheat oven to 350° F.

Divide the dough into 6 balls. Lightly dust a flat surface with flour. Using a rolling pin, roll each ball into a 5-inch circle. Gently press each circle into a tart pan, making the sides extend a bit higher than the pan. (The dough shrinks a bit during baking; this way the crust will be high enough to hold all the filling.) Prick the bottom of the dough with a fork, and bake for 10 minutes.

To make the filling: In a large sauté pan, cook the onion and garlic in the olive oil over moderate heat for 10 minutes, stirring frequently. Add the lamb, coriander, and fennel seed, and cook for 5 minutes, or until the meat loses its pink color. Add the tomatoes and sherry and bring to a boil over high heat. Reduce the heat to moderate and cook for 35 to 40 minutes, or until the liquids have evaporated, the meat is tender, and the mixture is fairly thick. Add the parsley and horseradish and cook for 2 to 3 minutes, stirring all the while. Remove from the heat and cool slightly. Add the cheese; mix well, and season with salt and pepper.

Fill each shell with the filling. Bake at 350° F. for 30 to 35 minutes or until the filling is hot and browned. Remove from the oven and serve immediately.

Dough:

1½ cups all-purpose flour

¼ teaspoon salt

4 tablespoons chilled vegetable shortening

4 tablespoons (½ stick) unsalted butter, cut into 6 pieces

2 to 3 tablespoons ice water

Filling:

1 large onion, cut in small dice

3 cloves garlic, minced

3 tablespoons olive oil

1 pound lamb stew meat, finely chopped (not minced or ground)

1 teaspoon each ground coriander and fennel seed

1½ cups chopped tomatoes

¾ cup dry sherry

1 cup chopped parsley

6-inch piece horseradish root, peeled and grated

½ pound feta cheese, crumbled

Salt and pepper, to taste

Horseradish-Stuffed Pork Loin

This stuffed pork loin makes an outstanding presentation. Have your butcher cut a "pocket" in the pork loin for the colorful stuffing. The recipe makes enough stuffing for two pork loins, or enough to fill one and to bake a separate dish of stuffing. With roasted new potatoes or rice, or the extra stuffing, and a green vegetable, this dish is good to serve for company, since it is easy and fast. Offer prepared horseradish alongside the roast if you yearn for more horseradish flavor. Makes 4 to 6 servings.   *Hot: rated 1*

½ **pound thick sliced bacon**

1 **large onion, cut in small dice**

3 **cloves garlic, minced**

4 **tablespoons (½ stick) unsalted butter**

2 **teaspoons each dried thyme, sage, and basil**

1 **large green apple, cored, and cut in small dice**

4-inch **piece horseradish root, peeled and minced**

¾ **cup dried cranberries or dried pitted cherries**

1 **cup Madeira**

2 **cups dried cornbread crumbs**

Salt and pepper, to taste

1 **2½-pound boned pork loin, with a pocket cut for stuffing**

1 **cup prepared horseradish (optional)**

Sage sprigs, for garnish

Preheat oven to 450° F.

In a large sauté pan, cook the bacon until it is crisp, remove with a slotted spoon, and drain on paper towels. Chop coarsely and place in a large bowl. Discard all but 3 tablespoons of the fat, and transfer this to a large, deep-sided skillet.

Cook the onion and garlic in the bacon fat over moderate heat for 15 minutes, stirring from time to time. Add the butter, spices, apple, horseradish, and cranberries and cook over moderate heat for 5 minutes. Add the Madeira and the cornbread crumbs and cook over high heat for 3 to 4 minutes, stirring all the while to mix the ingredients thoroughly. Remove from the heat, add to the bacon, mix well, and season with salt and pepper.

Place half of the stuffing in a small baking dish and cover with foil. Gently stuff the remainder into the pocket of the loin, pressing the stuffing all the way into the pocket and making the loin round with stuffing. Tie with kitchen string to secure the opening and keep the shape of the meat.

Fill a shallow baking pan with water to a depth of 2 inches. Place the pork loin on a flat roasting rack set inside the pan. Roast for 30 minutes at 450° F. Reduce the heat to 400° F. and roast for 20 to 25 minutes more, or until the meat has lost its pink color and the stuffing is hot. Do not overcook the meat or it will be tough, dry, and tasteless.

Let the pork stand at room temperature for 8 to 10 minutes before cutting. Slice into 1-inch rounds, garnish with sage sprigs, and serve immediately, with additional prepared horseradish if desired.

Three-Sausage Stew with Horseradish and Greens

2 large onions, cut in medium wedges

4 cloves garlic, thinly sliced

¼ cup olive oil

1 rounded teaspoon each dried thyme, oregano, basil, and rosemary

2 cups dry white wine

2 cups chopped and seeded tomatoes

6-inch piece fresh horseradish root, peeled and finely chopped

½ pound hot Polish sausage, cut in ½-inch rounds

1 pound sweet Italian sausage, cut in ½-inch rounds

1 pound garlic sausage, cut in ½-inch rounds

1 large bunch Swiss chard, stemmed and very coarsely chopped

Salt and pepper, to taste

Fresh herb sprigs, for garnish

Fresh horseradish root adds texture to this hearty meat-lover's stew, while complementing flavorful sausages. The horseradish loses much of its pungency through cooking, adding just the right zing to this cold-weather dish. Serve with country-style bread, baked potatoes or noodles, and dark beer.
Makes 4 to 6 servings.   *Hotter: rated 6*

In a large deep-sided pan, cook the onions and garlic in the olive oil over moderate heat for 15 to 20 minutes, stirring frequently. Add the herbs and 1 cup of the wine and cook for 10 minutes over high heat. Add tomatoes, horseradish, sausages, and remaining wine and cook for 5 minutes over high heat.

Reduce the heat to moderate and cook for 15 minutes, or until the sausages are tender and cooked. Do not overcook the sausages or they will be dry and tough. Add the Swiss chard just before serving, or ladle the stew onto a bed of the greens. Season with salt and pepper, and garnish with fresh herb sprigs.

Beef and Watercress Sandwiches with Horseradish Cream Cheese

I remember my Mom telling me about the watercress sandwiches she had at a bridge party 50 years ago—watercress, butter, and white bread. That isn't my idea of great food, much less lunch, but I think these sandwiches could qualify as a real meal. If you are pressed for time you can buy sliced roast beef, making just the cream cheese at home.
Makes about 6 servings.

Hotter: rated 4

2 tablespoons olive oil

1½ pounds filet mignon, trimmed of excess fat

1 pound natural cream cheese (no gums or preservatives)

5- to 6-inch piece horseradish root, peeled and grated

⅓ cup minced chives

Black pepper, to taste

1 large bunch watercress, stemmed

12 slices firm whole wheat or country-style bread

Whole chives, for garnish

Yellow cherry tomatoes, for garnish

Heat the olive oil in a sauté pan large enough to accommodate the steaks. When the oil is hot, add the meat and cook over moderately high heat for 2 to 3 minutes per side, or until the meat is medium rare and the outside is browned. Remove from the pan and let stand at room temperature for 10 minutes before slicing. Slice into thin pieces and set aside until needed.

Meanwhile, combine the cream cheese, horseradish, minced chives, and black pepper in a small bowl. Spread each slice of bread with some of the cream cheese mixture. Top half the slices with a few sprigs of watercress. Arrange some slices of beef on top of the watercress, and cover with a few more sprigs of watercress and the second slice of bread. Press gently to secure the ingredients and garnish with the whole chives and yellow cherry tomatoes. Serve at room temperature.

Hangover Bloody Marys

Jalapeño Pepper Vodka:

1 quart vodka

2 fresh jalapeño peppers, halved

1 quart tomato juice

¾ cup prepared horseradish

¼ cup Worcestershire sauce

¼ cup fresh lime juice

3 tablespoons Tabasco sauce

1 tablespoon each ground celery seed and black pepper

1 teaspoon ground cinnamon

Stalks of celery, trimmed

Lime slices

If in fact you are suffering from a hangover, it might be best to have someone else prepare this mix! On the other hand, if you expect a hangover, make the mix the night before—it will taste even better the second day. If you want to use regular vodka for the cocktails, feel free, but this special peppery version is sensational in Bloody Marys (and even better taken straight from a frozen shot glass). A less traditional garnish would be a pickled jalapeño slit to the stem on the rim of each glass.
Mix makes 4 to 6 servings.   *Hottest: rated 7*

To make the Jalapeño Pepper Vodka: Place the two jalapeño peppers in a bottle of vodka for 2 to 4 days, depending on how hot you like your vodka. Remove the peppers and the vodka is ready to drink. (If you leave the peppers in the vodka indefinitely, the vodka will get hotter and hotter.)

Combine the tomato juice, horseradish, Worcestershire sauce, lime juice, Tabasco sauce, and the spices; mix well and adjust seasoning. Pour the mix into glasses filled with ice cubes, leaving enough room for the vodka. Generally, 1 to 1½ ounces of liquor per 6 ounces of mix is used, but in the case of a hangover as little as a drop or as much as 3 ounces of liquor could be in order. Garnish each glass with a sprinkling of pepper and one stalk of celery or a lime slice. Serve immediately if not sooner.

PEPPER, KING OF THE SPICE TRADE, IS THE DRIED FRUIT OF A TROPICAL vine native to India. This singular spice dominated the European spice trade through the Middle Ages, and was considered as precious as gold. (Like mustard and other strong spices, it was originally used to mask the aging or outright rancid taste of bad food.) It wasn't uncommon then in Europe for the spice to be traded for rent or taxes, and pepper eventually became so expensive that herbs and less-precious spices took its place in the kitchen.

Pepper is grown today in southern India, Cambodia, eastern Asia, the West Indies, Madagascar, and Brazil. *Piper longum*, or long pepper, is a related plant referred to in Sanskrit as *pippali*, and it is from this word that we get our name for the spice. The countries that produce peppercorns use a vast quantity of several different types, both fresh and dried, and all cuisines use at least one kind of pepper in almost every dish.

Black pepper is picked as a green or unripe berry. It is dried in the sun for eight to ten days and shrinks and shrivels until hard, dry, and black. There are many varieties of black pepper, each with a distinctive taste and aroma, but generally speaking black peppercorns are pungent in aroma and flavor, and can add a great deal of heat.

White pepper is picked ripe and has been soaked in water to facilitate removing the outer skin. After the skin is rubbed off, the gray inner peppercorn is dried until it turns a light tan color. Smaller than most black peppercorns, it has a milder taste but can still add depth and heat. When color is a consideration and black "specks" are inappropriate in a particular dish, ground white pepper often is used instead of black.

Green peppercorns are picked unripe, and usually preserved in brine. In dried form, they are dry, of course, but can be used just like the black, white, or dried pink peppercorns. Preserved by either method, they have an invigorating, lively taste and are used primarily in sauces and relatively delicate dishes. Fresh green berries still on the stem, though not called for here, are often used in Southeast Asian cuisine, and they can be especially pungent in this form.

Pink or red peppercorns are picked nearly ripe, and come mainly from the South American tree *Schinus terebinthifolius*. These rosy colored peppercorns are fairly brittle and soft when dried. (They may be referred to as either pink or red in market form but are the same berry.) Pink peppercorns are milder in flavor, are aromatic rather than hot, and are less intense than the black, white, or green ones. Both pink and green peppercorns are quite expensive.

When purchasing dried pepper, look for whole peppercorns that are sold in a tightly sealed container. Peppercorns are often sold in bulk in natural food stores, spice and specialty food shops, and ethnic markets. This is an excellent and economical way to buy this spice, as long as the pepper is fresh. To check, rub a few peppercorns between your fingers and sniff for a pronounced aroma. If the spices are old they will be lacking in flavor and character, and will add little to your food. Black and white pepper are sold ground as well, but under no circumstance should you purchase this form. Pre-ground varieties often include fillers and other unwanted ingredients and are usually stale; they lack the intensity, flavor, and quality of whole peppercorns.

You may grind your own dried peppercorns in a pepper mill, or an electric spice or coffee grinder, or with a mortar and pestle, or a hand mill. I like to use a sturdy metal pepper mill for cooking and another for the table. An adjustable mill is preferable, so that you can select and adjust the texture and size of the pepper; fine, medium, and coarsely ground pepper each have a place in cooking, as well as at the table. It is convenient to have a small mortar and pestle for coarse grinding and bruising.

Finely ground pepper—ground until it can't get any finer—is used for a more subtle flavoring effect, and when visible pepper bits are undesirable. Medium grind is most versatile, and can be used in most dishes as well as at the table. Coarsely ground pepper is most often dispensed from pepper mills at the table for salads or soup, and sometimes entrées, but it can be and is used in the kitchen as well. Closest to the whole form are peppercorns that are not really ground but somewhat split, sometimes halved, or bruised. Whole dried peppercorns are usually used in stock and pickling compounds. In a few of the recipes that follow they're cooked or used as garnish as whole peppercorns—a form that hotheads will savor.

To bruise peppercorns in a mortar and pestle, place the spice in the center of the mortar and lightly rub with the pestle until the desired texture is achieved. To bruise or grind without a pepper mill, mortar and pestle, or electric grinder; place the spice in a medium-sized bowl, and use a smaller bowl that will fit inside it to rub and crush the peppercorns. You may also place the peppercorns on a cutting board and press gently (until they are bruised) with a heavy skillet or rolling pin. If you try to bruise or crush the peppercorns too aggressively at first they will fly all over the room. Be gentle until they are bruised and then, if desired, you can use more force to grind them smaller.

Avocado Soup with Green Peppercorns

1 medium onion, cut in medium dice

2 cloves garlic, minced

1 tablespoon ground coriander

1 teaspoon ground cumin

¼ cup olive oil

4 large ripe avocados, peeled, pitted, and coarsely chopped

2½ quarts light chicken stock

⅓ cup green peppercorns in brine, drained (reserve a few for garnish)

Salt and pepper, to taste

Cilantro leaves, for garnish

Rich, velvety, and smooth, this spring or summer soup can be served hot or cold, and is delicious with warm tortillas or tortilla chips served with tomato salsa cruda and fresh Mexican cheese. The piquant green peppercorns in brine balance the richness of the avocados and add just the right amount of zing.
Makes about 6 servings.   *Hotter: rated 4*

In a large saucepan, cook the onion, garlic, and spices in the olive oil over moderate heat for 10 minutes, stirring frequently. Add the avocados and chicken stock and bring to a boil over high heat. Reduce the heat to moderate and cook for 20 minutes. Cool to room temperature.

Purée the soup mixture in a blender until very smooth. Transfer back to the saucepan and bring to a boil over high heat. Add the peppercorns and salt and pepper. Reduce the heat to moderate and cook for 10 minutes. Serve with a garnish of cilantro and a few peppercorns.

Lobster-Grapefruit Salad with Pink Peppercorns

Ultimately elegant and refined, this special occasion salad is ideal for a light warm-weather supper, served with champagne or a crisp sauvignon blanc. If you can't find lobster tails, use jumbo prawns instead.
Makes 4 to 6 servings.   Hot: rated 2

Using kitchen scissors or a very sharp knife, remove the lobster meat from the shells. Save the shells for making stock or discard. Place the lobster meat and the wine in a shallow saucepan. Bring to a boil over high heat, reduce the heat to moderate, and cook for 2 to 3 minutes or until the lobster is just done. Do not overcook the lobster meat. Remove with a slotted spoon and cool to room temperature, reserving the wine.

When the meat is cool enough to handle, slice it into ½-inch rounds and arrange around the inner edge of a large plate. Arrange the grapefruit fillets between the slices of lobster.

To make the vinaigrette: Place the shallots in the reserved wine and bring to a boil over high heat. Boil until liquid is reduced to 2 table-spoons. Place in a large bowl and cool to room temperature. Using a wire whisk, incorporate small amounts of the olive oil, whisking all the while. Slowly add the grapefruit juice and vinegar, whisking all the while to form a smooth emulsion. Add the peppercorns; mix well and season with salt.

Place the endive in a bowl and dress with half of the vinaigrette; mix gently. Arrange endive in a mound in the center of the lobster and grapefruit. Drizzle the lobster and grapefruit with the remaining vinaigrette, and serve at room temperature.

Note: To cut citrus fruit into fillets, use a very sharp paring knife to first peel the fruit, taking care to remove all the pith. Then cut between the fibers that separate each section in order to remove the pulp, leaving behind the white membrane. Gently lay each fillet on a flat surface as you remove it from the whole fruit.

4 lobster tails (about 1 pound each in the shell)

1 cup white wine

2 large pink grapefruits, cut into fillets (see Note)

Vinaigrette:

2 shallots, peeled and thinly sliced

1 cup olive oil

2 tablespoons grapefruit juice

2 tablespoons champagne vinegar

2½ tablespoons red peppercorns, bruised

Salt, to taste

2 firm heads endive, trimmed and slivered

Mussels and Prawns with Orange-Pink Peppercorn Vinaigrette

This warm salad of fresh mussels and prawns is elegant and light, and at its best when served with a toasty champagne or a buttery chardonnay. You might serve the seafood on a bed of rocket or baby greens as well as with angel hair pasta. Makes 4 servings.

Hot: rated 2

Bring a large pot of water to boil over high heat. When the water is boiling, add the prawns and cook for 1 minute. Drain and rinse with cold water. When the prawns are cool enough to handle, remove the shells and tails. Place in a bowl.

Scrub the shells of the mussels and remove the beards. Place the mussels and the wine in a shallow skillet. Bring to a boil over high heat, cover, reduce the heat to moderate, and cook for 4 to 5 minutes, or until all the shells have opened. Remove all those that have opened, and cook the remaining mussels in the wine for 2 minutes. Discard any that have not opened. When the opened shells are cool enough to handle, remove the mussels and add to the prawns.

To make the vinaigrette: place the orange juice, saffron, and peppercorns in a small saucepan. Over moderate heat, stir constantly until the orange juice is hot and the saffron is soft, 4 to 5 minutes. Remove from the heat and cool to room temperature.

Place the walnut oil and garlic in a bowl. Slowly add the champagne vinegar, whisking all the while to form a smooth emulsion. Add the orange juice mixture slowly, whisking all the while. Season with salt and pepper.

Add the vinaigrette to the seafood and mix gently. Arrange around the buttered pasta, or on top of greens, and garnish with the chives.

½ pound medium-sized prawns

12-15 mussels (make sure the shells are closed when you buy them)

1 cup dry white wine

Vinaigrette:

3 tablespoons orange juice

1 teaspoon saffron

3 tablespoons pink peppercorns

¾ cup walnut oil

1 clove garlic, minced

2 tablespoons champagne vinegar

Salt and pepper, to taste

½ cup chopped fresh chives, for garnish

Chive blossoms (optional), for garnish

Vietnamese Salt and Pepper Prawns

1 pound jumbo prawns

2 tablespoons each coarsely ground black and Szechuan peppercorns

2 tablespoons Kosher or other coarse salt

1 tablespoon sugar

4 cloves garlic, minced

¼ cup homemade beef stock or unsalted beef broth

3 tablespoons *nuoc cham* (fish sauce)

3 tablespoons fresh lime juice

Traditionally, these prawns are served in the shell as they are described here in this recipe. The action of the salt and pepper (along with the liquid flavoring ingredients) serves as a tenderizer and reduces cooking time considerably. Cooking in the shell is best, but if you simply can't stand to peel your own shrimp at the table, remove the shells first (leaving the tails intact) and proceed with the recipe. Serve this simple seafood dish with stir-fried vegetables, noodles or rice, and perhaps a Vietnamese beef or vegetable salad.
Makes 4 servings.   Hot: rated 3

Combine all the ingredients in a nonreactive bowl and mix well. Let stand at room temperature for 1 hour, or in the refrigerator for up to 24 hours.

Preheat oven to 450° F.

Transfer the prawns and the marinade to a baking pan. Bake for 5 minutes. Remove from oven and serve prawns immediately.

Four-Peppercorn Filet Mignon

For a classic French bistro supper serve this peppery filet with French-fried potatoes. Baked or pan-fried potatoes are also a good complement, and a green salad or broccoli makes this a simple, balanced dinner.
Makes 4 servings.   *Hotter: rated 4*

Combine the peppercorns, salt, and olive oil in a shallow dish; mix well. Coat each piece of meat with this mixture, taking care to coat both sides equally.

Set a nonstick skillet that is just large enough to accommodate the steaks over high heat. When the skillet is hot, add the steaks. Reduce the heat to moderately high and cook on the first side for 2 to 3 minutes. Carefully flip the steaks and continue cooking on the other side. The total cooking time depends on how you like your meat cooked. I suggest medium rare.

Remove the steaks to a large platter and keep warm in a low oven while you prepare the sauce. Remove the leftover peppercorns and oil from the skillet and return it to the heat.

Add the garlic and brandy to the skillet and cook over high heat for 1 minute. Add the cream and cook over high heat, stirring all the while, until it is thick enough to coat the back of a spoon, 3 to 4 minutes. Drizzle the sauce over the meat and serve immediately.

2 tablespoons each pink, green, white, and black peppercorns, lightly crushed

2 teaspoons Kosher or other coarse salt

2 tablespoons olive oil

4 8-ounce filet mignon steaks, trimmed of excess fat

6 cloves garlic, minced

½ cup brandy or cognac

1 cup heavy cream

Chinese Braised Short Ribs with Black Pepper

These ultratender beef ribs are at once peppery and slightly sweet. Served with stir-fried green vegetables and steamed rice, these ribs make an unforgettable meal for those who enjoy the intense flavors of Chinese cuisine.
Makes 4 servings.   *Hotter: rated 5*

In a deep-sided pan, cook the ribs in the peanut oil over high heat until they are browned on all sides. Add the garlic, ginger, peppercorns, and anise, and cook for 1 minute. Add the red wine and continue cooking until it evaporates. Add the beef stock, soy sauce, oyster sauce, vinegar, and brown sugar and bring to a boil.

Reduce the heat to moderately low; cover and cook for 1 hour or until the meat is very tender and the sauce is thick and aromatic. Using a spoon, remove the excess fat from the sauce. Add all but 2 tablespoons of the green onions; mix gently. Garnish with the remaining green onions, and with the star anise and kumquats if desired.

2 pounds English short ribs, cut in 2-inch lengths

2 tablespoons peanut oil

4 cloves garlic, thinly sliced

1-inch piece ginger root, peeled and minced

2 tablespoons each coarsely ground black and Szechuan peppercorns

3 star anise (more for garnish, if desired)

1 cup dry red wine

2 cups homemade beef stock or unsalted beef broth

¼ cup soy sauce

3 tablespoons oyster sauce

3 tablespoons Chinese black vinegar

2 tablespoons brown sugar

1 small bunch green onions, trimmed and minced (reserve some for garnish)

Kumquats, for garnish (optional)

Figs with White Peppercorn Syrup and Basil

½ cup white peppercorns, bruised

1 large bunch fresh basil (stems included), coarsely chopped

3 cups water

1 cup white wine

2 cups sugar

2 cups dried black figs, stemmed

2 tablespoons whole white peppercorns, for garnish

6 sprigs basil or mint, for garnish

Lavender, or other edible flowers, for garnish

The recipe calls for dried figs, but if fresh are in season feel free to use them instead. If serving fresh figs, make the syrup according to the recipe, but add the fresh figs to the finished syrup just before serving. This sweet-peppery dessert is delicious and light on its own, and richer served with ice cream or pound cake. Makes 4 to 6 servings. Hotter: rated 6

Place the bruised peppercorns, basil, water, and wine in a heavy-bottomed saucepan. Bring to a boil over high heat, and continue boiling for 10 minutes. Add the sugar and return to a boil. Cook over high heat for 15 to 20 minutes, or until the liquid is thick and syrupy. Strain through a fine wire mesh and return to the saucepan.

Add the figs to the syrup and cook over moderate heat for 10 to 15 minutes or until the figs are very tender. Serve warm with some of the syrup and garnish with the whole peppercorns, sprigs of basil or mint, and optionally with edible flowers.

Port-Poached Dried Fruits with Black Pepper

This dish is ideal for fall or winter desserts, or for a heartwarming breakfast or brunch. The spicy compote is also good with roasted pork or lamb or with ice cream, accompanied by chunks of bittersweet chocolate or a simple butter or chocolate cake, or drizzled with crème fraîche.
Makes about 6 servings.   Hot: rated 3

1 bottle (750 ml) port

2 cups water

1 cup sugar

¼ cup black peppercorns

1 cup dried figs, stemmed and halved

1 cup dried apricots

½ cup pitted prunes

½ cup dried apple rings, halved (or quartered if large)

½ cup dried pineapple rings, quartered

½ cup dried cherries or cranberries

3 tablespoons vanilla extract

Mint sprigs, for garnish

Place the port, water, sugar, and peppercorns in a heavy-bottomed saucepan. Bring to a boil over high heat, stirring frequently; boil for 20 minutes or until the liquid begins to thicken and become syrupy. Add all the fruit, reduce the heat to moderate, cover, and cook for 15 to 20 minutes or until the fruit is tender but not mushy.

Add the vanilla; mix well and serve warm or at room temperature in shallow bowls. Garnish with a sprig of mint.

Braised Duck with Green Peppercorns and Prunes

1 pound bacon

1 pound small boiling onions, trimmed and peeled (see Note)

6 duck legs (about 4 pounds)

1 cup all-purpose flour

2 teaspoons each dried thyme, rosemary, and sage

1 cup dry sherry

2 quarts chicken stock (preferably homemade)

1⅓ cups pitted prunes, coarsely chopped

¼ cup coarsely ground green peppercorns

¼ cup whole green peppercorns in brine, drained

Salt and pepper, to taste

¾ cup chopped parsley, for garnish

Slightly sweet and piquant, this French-inspired duck stew is rich and robust. It's terrific served with grilled or soft polenta, wild rice, or pasta. To save time, you may use frozen pearl onions rather than fresh.
Makes 4 to 6 servings.   Hot: rated 3

In a very large sauté pan, cook the bacon until almost crisp. Remove with a slotted spoon, reserving the fat, and drain on paper towels. When cool, coarsely chop and place in a large bowl.

Cook the onions in the bacon fat over moderate heat for 8 to 10 minutes, stirring from time to time, until they are golden brown on all sides. Remove with a slotted spoon and add to the bacon. Transfer ¼ cup of the fat to a deep, heavy-bottomed saucepan. Discard the remaining fat.

Dredge the duck legs in the flour, making sure they are coated on all sides. Heat the bacon fat. When the fat is hot, add the duck legs and brown on all sides over moderate heat. Add the herbs and sherry and cook over high heat until the liquid almost evaporates, 4 to 5 minutes. Add 6 cups of the chicken stock and bring to a boil. Reduce the heat to moderate and cook until the duck is very tender and the liquid has almost evaporated, about 1½ hours.

Using a slotted spoon, remove the duck legs from the liquid and place in a colander. When cool enough to handle, remove the meat from the bones, taking care to remove the skin, tendons, and fat from the meat.

Add the chunks of meat to the bacon and onions, along with the prunes and peppercorns. Return to the cooking liquid along with the remaining 2 cups of chicken stock. Bring to a boil over high heat, reduce the heat to moderate, and cook for 25 to 30 minutes or until the liquid is slightly thickened and the stew is hot. Season with salt and pepper and garnish with the chopped parsley.

Note: To loosen the skin of fresh pearl onions, blanch in boiling water for 1 minute; drain, and cool slightly. Use a paring knife to remove the skin and trim the stem ends.

Four-Peppercorn Spice Butter

Use this flavorful, slightly sweet butter for vegetables; to melt on top of grilled or broiled fish, poultry, or meat; or to toss with hot pasta as a simple sauce. Mixed with garlic, this butter would make an intriguing peppery spread for toast. Makes ¼ pound seasoned butter.   *Hot: rated 2*

¼ pound (1 stick) unsalted butter, softened

2 teaspoons coarsely ground allspice

1½ teaspoons each ground green, pink, white, black peppercorns

½ teaspoon salt

Combine the above ingredients in a small bowl; mix well. You may store the butter in a covered container in the refrigerator for up to 1 week. Alternately, form it into a cylinder, wrap in wax or parchment paper, and freeze; slice rounds as needed.

LONG KNOWN FOR CHEST COLD RELIEF, MUSTARD HAS ALSO BEEN claimed to promote hair growth; it has been used for medicinal as well as culinary purposes for at least centuries and likely for millennia. The Greeks put mustard to both uses, but it was the Romans who turned the hard seeds into edible pastes by mixing them with vinegars, honey, spices, and nuts. When the Romans moved into Gaul they took the seeds with them, scattering the tiny round seeds along the way.

Over time, Burgundy became the center of European mustard production, and Dijon, still one of the leading areas for production, became the center of trade. In 1777 Monsieur Grey and Monsieur Poupon founded a mustard-making company; to this day, the French city of Dijon is responsible for producing nearly all the mustard eaten in France. In Britain, two women independently perfected mustard making in the 1700s, but it was Jeremiah Colman who, opening a factory in the early 1800s, took the mustard seed and ran with it. The same factory still produces mustard powder with the name Colman.

The mustard we use in cooking is derived from seeds of the *Cruciferae* family. Mustard plants are annuals and always produce bright yellow flowers. Black mustard originated in the Middle East and Asia, but it has been cultivated in Europe for centuries. The seeds were used primarily before 1930; due to the difficulty of harvesting the seed, black mustard was ruled out as a viable crop for mass production. Brown mustard seed, which was developed in part because of that difficulty, has now become more popular than its black counterpart. Originally an Asian plant, it now grows throughout northern Europe and in parts of England, and is favored by many mustard makers who produce a flavorful, pungent mustard. The seed is, however, less pungent than the black and is often combined with the milder yellow seed. Native to the Mediterranean, yellow mustard seed is now grown in eastern counties of England and in the United States. The seeds are actually pale yellow, and they are larger than the black and brown seeds and less pungent yet. They are used primarily in English and American mustards and are ground and sold as mustard powder. (Black mustard seeds are difficult to find in the United States, so I suggest using brown and yellow.)

The outer husks of mustard seeds contain mucilage, a sticky gumlike substance. When the seeds are crushed and mixed with water, the enzyme myrosin and the glucoside contained in the seeds form a volatile oil that gives mustard its intense pungency. Myrosin reacts badly to boiling water, leaving a bitter and unpleasant taste to the finished product, so use cold water when preparing mustard at home. Preparing mustard is simple and fun, and all you really need is an electric or hand spice-grinder and an assortment of mustard seeds, or just dry mustard, and some interesting vinegars, spices, and herbs.

When purchasing mustard seeds, look for regular, even-colored, hard seeds. They won't have any aroma in this form, but when they are crushed or bruised the aroma of the oil released will be powerful. To store the seeds, enclose them in a plastic bag in a cool, dark place, for up to one year. Purchase powdered mustard in a sealed can rather than in bulk. Powder in bulk tends to lose its strength and intensity, becoming stale if there isn't a great demand for it at a particular store. I like Colman's dried mustard powder and use it in cooking and for preparing mustards.

When cooking with mustard, remember that as with horseradish, ginger, and some chilies, the pungency is lost with long cooking or high heat. Generally speaking, it is best to add mustard at the end of cooking rather than at the beginning. Mustard pastes are a natural thickener, and since mustard is so low in calories and fat, it is a sensible and delicious thickening agent for many dishes. Use smooth mustard for delicate or light-colored sauces, and coarse-grained for heartier and more robust and rustic dishes. Honey mustard contains more sugar than regular mustards and tends to caramelize when heated. If you have coated the outside of a piece of meat or poultry with honey mustard, remember that the exterior may looked cooked, or even burned, if you are not careful, while the interior is still undercooked.

There are now thousands of commercial mustards on the market, one fancier than the next. Some are overpriced and too muddy in flavor. Most store-bought mustards are quite good, however, and are terrific to have around for spreading on bread and crackers, for serving with cheese, dried and cured meats, poultry, and fish, and for cooking. French, German, English, Dutch, and American, mustards vary in preparation, ingredients, texture, taste, and aroma, but they all have one thing in common—big flavor and versatility in the kitchen.

Indian Mango Chutney with Mustard

Mango gives this chutney a wonderful golden color, and the abundance of mustard seeds adds texture, color, and punch. For extra heat add the optional prepared hot mustard, but I suggest you taste the chutney before doing so. Serve with vegetable or meat dishes, as well as poultry, as pictured here.
Makes about 2½ cups.   *Hot: rated 3*

In a large sauté pan, cook the onion and jalapeño peppers in the oil over moderate heat for 10 minutes, stirring frequently. Add the garlic, spices, and vinegar and cook for 5 minutes, stirring constantly. Add the mango and lime juice; mix well. Reduce the heat to moderate, and cook for 5 minutes or until the fruit is soft and the mixture is aromatic.

Season the chutney with salt and pepper and taste it for heat; add the prepared hot mustard if desired. Cool to room temperature. Unless serving immediately, store in a covered glass or plastic container in the refrigerator. The chutney will keep for up to 1 month.

1 large onion, cut in small dice

2 jalapeño peppers, minced

3 tablespoons vegetable oil or unsalted butter

3 cloves garlic, minced

3 tablespoons yellow mustard seeds

2 teaspoons each ground coriander, turmeric, and whole black mustard seeds

1 teaspoon each ground cardamom, cumin, and cinnamon

⅓ cup white wine or apple cider vinegar

2 cups finely chopped peeled mango (about 2 large mangoes)

¼ cup fresh lime juice

Salt and pepper, to taste

2 tablespoons prepared hot mustard (optional)

Classic Potato Salad with Mustard Dressing

½ pound thick sliced bacon

1 large onion, cut in small dice

Mustard Dressing:

½ cup Dijon mustard

3 cloves garlic, minced

½ cup olive oil

¼ cup sherry vinegar

1 tablespoon brown mustard seeds

1½ pounds tiny new potatoes, halved

¼ cup capers, drained

1 small red pepper, cut into small triangles

Salt and pepper, to taste

1 small bunch mustard greens, trimmed

Tiny new potatoes, smokey bacon, and assertive mustard form the backbone of this traditional potato salad, but crisp, refreshing red peppers and bright-tasting mustard greens add a startling new twist.
Makes 4 servings.   Hot: rated 3

Cook the bacon in a large skillet until crisp. Remove with a slotted spoon and drain on paper towels. When cool enough to handle, chop coarsely and place in a large bowl. Set aside until needed.

Cook the onion in the remaining bacon fat over moderate heat for 15 minutes. Remove with a slotted spoon and add to the bacon.

To make the Mustard Dressing: Place the mustard and garlic in a bowl; mix well. Using a wire whisk, incorporate the olive oil a bit at a time, whisking all the while to form a smooth emulsion. Add the vinegar and whisk until smooth. Add the mustard seeds and mix well.

Meanwhile, cook the potatoes in salted boiling water until they are tender but not mushy. Drain in a colander and cool slightly. Add the potatoes to the bacon and onion and mix gently. Add the dressing, capers, and red pepper, and mix gently. Season with salt and pepper and serve on a bed of mustard greens.

Indian Lentils with
Brown Mustard Seeds and Mango

This traditional Indian lentil dish gets heat from both mustard seeds and prepared mustard. The slightly sweet flavor and velvety texture of the mango adds an uncommon and welcome flavor to the spicy lentils. Serve with basmati rice and chutney and two or three vegetable side dishes for a vegetarian meal, or serve with roasted meats or poultry.
Makes 4 to 6 servings.   *Hotter: rated 4*

Cook the onion, garlic, mustard seeds, and spices in the olive oil and butter over high heat for 5 minutes, stirring frequently. Set aside until needed.

Meanwhile, place the lentils and water in a large pot. Bring to a boil over high heat. Reduce the heat to moderate, add the onion spice mixture, and mix well. Simmer for 45 minutes or until the lentils are tender and the mixture is slightly soupy. Add the mango and mustard, season with salt and pepper and garnish with the cilantro. Serve immediately.

2 medium onions, cut in small dice

4 cloves garlic, thinly sliced

½ cup brown mustard seeds

2 teaspoons each ground cumin and coriander

1 teaspoon each ground fennel seed, anise seed, and fenugreek

3 tablespoons olive oil

3 tablespoons unsalted butter

1½ cups brown lentils, sorted

1½ quarts water

2 large mangoes, peeled and seeded, cut in small dice

¼ cup prepared hot English mustard

Salt and pepper, to taste

¾ cup chopped cilantro leaves

White Bean–Smoked Chicken Salad with Mustard

This Tuscan-style white bean salad is ideal for a spring or summer picnic. Use a vegetable peeler to make thin shavings of Parmesan cheese for the garnish. To easily cut smoked turkey into small cubes, ask your butcher or deli person to make one thick slice for you.
Makes 4 servings.   Hot: rated 3

Soak the beans in plenty of water for 8 hours or overnight. Drain the beans and place them in a saucepan with the bay leaves. Add 2 quarts of fresh water and bring to a boil over high heat. Reduce the heat to moderately high, and cook for 45 minutes to 1 hour or until the beans are very tender but not mushy. (Meanwhile make the vinaigrette.) Drain and place in a large bowl. Add the smoked chicken and onion and mix gently.

To make the vinaigrette: Place the mustard and garlic in a bowl; mix well. Using a wire whisk, incorporate the olive oil and then the vinegar a little at a time, whisking to form a smooth emulsion. Add the mustard seeds, herbs, and salt and pepper; mix well.

Dress the salad with the vinaigrette and mix gently. Serve at room temperature on a bed of radicchio or inside big individual leaves, garnished with shavings of Parmesan cheese and rosemary sprigs.

1½ cups white navy beans, sorted

2 quarts water

2 bay leaves

1 cup diced smoked chicken or turkey (about ½ pound)

1 small red onion, halved and thinly sliced

Vinaigrette:

¼ cup Dijon mustard

2 cloves garlic, minced

¾ cup olive oil

⅓ cup sherry vinegar

2 tablespoons yellow mustard seeds

2 teaspoons each dried rosemary, thyme, and sage

Salt and pepper, to taste

1 large head radicchio, trimmed

2 ounces Parmesan cheese

Rosemary sprigs, for garnish

Country-Style French Sausage Ragout with Mustard

10 large shallots, trimmed and peeled

10 whole (peeled) cloves garlic

1½ tablespoons yellow mustard seeds

¼ cup olive oil or bacon fat

2 bay leaves

2 teaspoons each dried thyme and rosemary

1 cup white wine

8 small new potatoes, halved

1 large bunch small carrots, trimmed and peeled

2 cups unsalted beef stock or broth

¾ pound smoked sausage, cut into 1-inch pieces

¾ cup Dijon mustard

Salt and pepper, to taste

1 cup chopped parsley, for garnish

Flavorful yet simple, this herb-scented ragout takes less than an hour to prepare. It makes a terrific cold-weather supper served with a salad of bitter greens. Makes 4 servings.

Hot: rated 2

In a shallow pot, cook the shallots, garlic, and mustard seeds in the olive oil over moderate heat for 10 minutes, stirring occasionally. Add the herbs and wine and bring to a boil over high heat. Cook for 5 minutes, or until the liquid evaporates. Add the potatoes, carrots, and beef broth; return to a boil. Reduce the heat to moderate and cook for 20 minutes or until the vegetables are almost tender.

Add the sausage and mustard and cook for 5 to 7 minutes, or until the sauce is thick and the sausage is hot all the way through. Season with salt and pepper and garnish with chopped parsley.

Roast Lamb with Mustard Crust

1 2-pound rack of lamb, trimmed of excess fat and ready to carve

¾ cup fine dried bread crumbs

¼ cup Dijon mustard

¼ cup honey mustard

¼ cup yellow mustard seeds

2 tablespoons brown mustard seeds

4 cloves garlic, minced

1 tablespoon dried rosemary

¼ cup minced parsley

Juice from 1 lemon

Rosemary sprigs, for garnish

Serve this elegant dish with roasted potatoes, or polenta and asparagus, or sautéed Swiss chard for a special occasion. A good bottle of zinfandel or cabernet sauvignon would be a splendid addition.
Makes 4 servings.   Hot: rated 2

Preheat oven to 450° F.

Pat the lamb dry with a kitchen towel. Combine the remaining ingredients except the rosemary sprigs in a bowl; mix well. Coat the lamb with the mixture, taking care to cover all sides equally and evenly. Set lamb on a flat roasting rack inside a lightly greased baking pan.

Roast the meat for 15 to 20 minutes, or until medium rare. Remove from the oven and let stand at room temperature for 5 to 7 minutes before slicing. Garnish with the rosemary and serve immediately.

Honey-Mustard Marinated Grilled Pork Tenderloin

Honey Mustard:

½ cup Colman's mustard powder

2 tablespoons brown mustard seeds

3 tablespoons dry sherry

⅓ cup honey

Salt and pepper, to taste

Marinade:

¼ cup olive oil

3 cloves garlic, minced

You can use commercial honey mustard for this marinade, but I have included a recipe for making your own at home. It is simple and delicious, and making your own mustard is sure to impress your family and friends. Served with sweet potatoes wrapped in foil and cooked in warm coals, and green vegetables, corn, or a salad, this entrée is very easy to make and serve.
Makes 4 servings.   Hot: rated 2

To make the Honey Mustard: Place the Colman's mustard, mustard seeds, sherry, and honey in a small bowl; mix well until smooth. Cover with plastic and let sit at room temperature for 1 to 8 hours before tasting. Mix again and season with salt and pepper. Set aside until needed.

To make the marinade: Place the olive oil, garlic, mustard seeds, and coriander in a bowl. Use a wire whisk to incorporate the wine a bit at

3 tablespoons yellow mustard seeds

1 tablespoon ground coriander

¼ cup dry white wine

¾ cup **Honey Mustard**

1 pork tenderloin (about 1 pound), trimmed of excess fat

a time, whisking all while. Add the mustard, a bit at a time, and mix well to form a smooth emulsion.

Place the tenderloin in a plastic bag with the marinade, making sure that the marinade comes in contact with all sides of the meat. Marinate in the refrigerator for 4 hours or up to 2 days, rotating every 8 hours or so, or at room temperature for 1½ hours.

Prepare a charcoal grill. When it is medium hot (a light coating of gray ash will cover the coals), place the meat on the grill. Cook 12 to 15 minutes, brushing with the marinade as the tenderloin cooks. Do not overcook the meat or it will be tough and dry—it should be barely pink in the center. Remove from the grill and let stand at room temperature for 5 minutes before slicing into ¾-inch rounds.

Chicken Breasts in Mustard Cream Sauce

This rich chicken dish is excellent served with wild rice, or over pasta. Definitely a crowd pleaser, this entrée also requires only a few steps. Sautéed or steamed vegetables will complete the meal.
Makes 4 servings.   *Hot: rated 1*

4 medium-sized chicken breasts

3 cups heavy cream

2 cloves garlic, minced

2 tablespoons brown mustard seeds

1 teaspoon dried thyme

3 tablespoons Dijon mustard

3 tablespoons coarse-grained mustard

Salt and pepper, to taste

Parsley or fresh thyme, for garnish

Place the chicken breasts in a large pot and cover with water. Bring to a boil over high heat; boil for 10 minutes. Remove pot from the heat and let chicken stand for 10 minutes. Remove with a slotted spoon and cool slightly. When cool enough to handle, remove the meat from the bones, taking care to remove the tendons and fat. Set aside until needed.

In a 12- or 15-inch skillet, combine the cream, garlic, mustard seeds, and thyme. Bring to a boil over high heat, stirring constantly since heavy cream cooked over high heat tends to boil over. Cook for 8 to 10 minutes or until the cream is almost thick enough to coat the back of a spoon.

Add the reserved chicken and the mustards and mix well. Cook for 2 to 3 minutes or until the sauce is thick and the chicken is hot all the way through. Season with salt and pepper and garnish with parsley or thyme sprigs. Serve immediately.

Sardine and Coarse-Grained Mustard Sandwiches

Coarse-Grained Mustard:

⅓ cup yellow mustard seeds

2 tablespoons Colman's dry mustard powder

2 tablespoons apple cider vinegar

2 tablespoons water

3 tablespoons olive or vegetable oil

¼ cup soy sauce

2 teaspoons turmeric

Salt and pepper, to taste

4 to 5 tins sardines packed in oil

8 thick slices country-style rye, sourdough, or wheat bread

Escarole, frisée, curly endive, or leafy greens

¾ pound Havarti, Danbo, Gruyère, or any flavorful German or Danish cheese, thinly sliced

Spicy-hot mustard and pleasantly oily sardines are an ideal pairing. Choose a rustic, dense, and flavorful bread for this satisfying lunch or light supper dish, and serve it with ale or stout. You can use fresh sardines if you can find them, but the tinned variety is really quite tasty. Use your favorite commercial coarse-grained mustard if you don't want to make your own. If you would like to serve these sandwiches open-faced, use only 4 slices of bread, and follow the assembly directions for the regular sandwich, leaving off the last piece of bread. Makes 4 sandwiches.   *Hot: rated 3*

To make the Coarse-Grained Mustard: Place all the ingredients except the salt and pepper in a blender. Purée until well blended and the mixture forms a coarse paste. Season with salt and pepper and let stand, covered, at room temperature for 8 hours before using. The mustard improves and becomes less biting as it stands. Four or five days in the refrigerator will make the mustard milder.

Drain the sardines. Spread each slice of bread with the mustard. Arrange some greens on 4 slices of bread, top with a few slices of cheese, and cover with the sardines. Add a bit more greens, and top with the second slice of bread. Slice in half and serve at room temperature.

CHILIES ARE THE FRUITS OF PUNGENT SPECIES OF THE CAPSICUM genus, known as sweet or bell peppers, pimientos, and hot chili peppers. They often provoke a reaction from lips and fingertips even before they reach the palate. Certainly the most flamboyant of all the "heating" elements, they are also the most difficult to differentiate and classify.

Adopted in the late 1400s by Spanish settlers, chilies had been used by the Aztecs and Mayans in Central and South America and by the Indians in the West Indies for centuries. On Columbus's second journey, in 1495, the Spanish returned home with the plant, where it thrived in the hot, sunny climate of the Mediterranean. Portuguese and Spanish traders brought the chilies to Africa, India, and the Far East, where they were embraced with passion. Chilies are part of almost every cuisine today; many countries have practically built their diet around this intoxicating fruit.

Chili peppers are grown in hot, tropical climates from sea level to elevations of six thousand feet. Sweet peppers and some chilies grow in warm temperate zones as well, but generally speaking, the hotter the climate, the happier the fruit. India, Mexico, China, Japan, Indonesia, and Thailand are the major exporters, and the United States is one of the biggest importers. Outstanding sweet peppers are grown with great success in hothouses in Holland.

Compared to the other hot ingredients in this book, chilies don't have as long and illustrious a history in the medicine cabinet. Though they have been used to cure the common cold, for bronchial disorders, to treat stomach maladies, and perhaps most importantly against high blood pressure, in fact, too many chilies can burn the stomach lining as well as the intestines. Some say that hot peppers are an aphrodisiac, and can even be addicting.

Not all chili peppers are hot, and not all are red. Some are mild and almost sweet, while others seem hot enough to fuel a rocket. Chili peppers can range in color from pale green to yellow, orange, red, purple, brown, or black. Sizes range from the tiny birds-eye chili's half- to three-quarter-inch length to the large, rounded, plump bell pepper. In between we have, for example, the small jalapeño pepper, which can be as big around as a quarter and two inches long, and the fresh poblano, which is usually four to five inches long and about two inches across at the widest part. Generally speaking, the smaller the pepper the hotter it tastes. I believe that "starving" the pepper plant of water can result in hotter fruit, but this could be a home-gardener's myth. Dried chilies have lost some of their heat, but this slight lessening heightens other facets of their flavor. Chilies also come pickled, roasted, cooked and combined with spices, or packed in oil. In the event that fresh chilies are difficult to find, rest assured that the prepared ones are always better than none at all (and for a few recipes even preferable).

When purchasing fresh chili peppers look for fruit that is firm, smooth, free of blemishes, and even colored. Store fresh chilies in a plastic bag in the refrigerator for up to two weeks, depending on the chili, or at cool room temperature for the smaller varieties. Always refrigerate larger bell peppers and poblano and California chilies, as they are more perishable than the smaller varieties, and tend to show signs of age sooner. If you leave fresh chilies out too long, they begin to shrivel and dry. They are still usable in this state but have lost some of their kick. If you leave them too long they will dry completely—which is fine if you want dried chili peppers. If this happens by accident, simply store the completely dried chilies in a tightly sealed jar or container at room temperature. Predried commercial chilies can be stored in the same way or even in a paper bag. Most dried chilies can be stored for several years in a cool, dry, dark place.

When cooking with chilies the first thing to know is that the oils from the fruit can burn your skin and mucous membranes. Some people like to wear gloves, but I like to tough it out and just keep my hands out of my eyes for a while. Washing your hands with hot water and soap removes a little bit of the oil, but only time will really do the trick. The skin, seeds, and ribs of the chili contain the most capsicum, and therefore are the hottest part of the fruit. If you want less heat then remove the seeds and ribs. Certain dishes are marred by the appearance of seeds and require seeding for that reason alone. (Always remove the stems, as they are hard and inedible.) All chilies are hotter when eaten raw, and most lose some pungency when cooked for a long period of time. Some say that raw salsas get hotter as they sit, but I have never found this to be true.

There are over four hundred different varieties of chili peppers; cataloging them here would be out of the question. Predicting the heat intensity of even one variety of pepper is nearly impossible, since one batch of jalapeño peppers at the local market could be mild, while the next could

Besides being used in their raw form, fresh chili peppers can be cooked, roasted, or pickled. To roast a chili pepper over a gas flame: hold it over the flame with kitchen tongs, rotating the pepper as the skin just begins to turn black in each area. When it is completely black, place it in a plastic bag, seal tightly, and allow it to "steam" for one hour or overnight. It can then be peeled under running water to aid in removing all the charred skin, as well as seeded and stemmed. At this point roasted peppers can be stored in the refrigerator in a plastic bag for a couple of days, pickled in spiced vinegar, or packed in oil and refrigerated for up to one month. You can also roast chili peppers on a charcoal grill, but take care to rotate them as the skin blackens. Intense heat can blacken the flesh as well, leaving nothing to eat but charred fruit.

be incendiary. The only way to tell if one particular chili is hot is to sample it raw. Finally, remember that what is stimulating and delicious for you may be intolerable for your guests.

Chili Shrimp Corn Cakes with Chipotle Mayonnaise

These golden brown shrimp and corn cakes are made with fresh and dried chilies and are served with a fiery mayonnaise made with smoked and dried jalapeños called chipotle peppers. Find these dried chili peppers in bulk in natural food stores or in Latin markets. They are also sold canned in adobo sauce. I prefer to buy them in the sauce as they have extra flavor and are already reconstituted.
Makes 4 to 6 servings (12 cakes)   *Hotter: rated 5*

Chipotle Mayonnaise:

2 egg yolks

2 cloves garlic, minced

⅓ cup vegetable oil

⅓ cup olive oil

2 tablespoons fresh lime juice

1½ tablespoons minced chipotle peppers (see Note)

Salt and pepper, to taste

Chili Shrimp Corn Cakes:

3 dried ancho or pasilla chilies

¾ pound small prawns

2 jalapeño peppers, seeded, stemmed, and minced

1 tablespoon ground coriander

1½ cups fresh corn kernels (about 2 ears of corn)

To make the Chipotle Mayonnaise: Place the egg yolks and garlic in a small bowl. Slowly add the vegetable oil, drop by drop, incorporating it all the while with a wire whisk to form a smooth emulsion. When all the vegetable oil has been added, slowly add the olive oil in a thin stream, whisking all the while. Add the lime juice and chipotle pepper: mix well. Season with salt and pepper and store in the refrigerator, covered, until needed.

To make the Chili Shrimp Corn Cakes: Soak the dried chilies in boiling water to cover for 2 to 3 hours or until soft and pliable. Remove the seeds and stems, and mince. Place in a large bowl and set aside until needed.

Bring a large pot of water to a boil over high heat. Add the prawns and cook for 1 minute. Remove, drain, and rinse with cold water. When the prawns are cool enough to handle, remove shells and tails. Finely chop and add to the chilies.

Cook the jalapeño pepper, coriander, and corn in the olive oil over moderate heat for 5 minutes, stirring frequently. Add the green onions and cilantro and cook for 2 minutes over high heat, stirring constantly. Remove from the pan and add to the prawns and chilies; mix well and cool to room temperature. Add the sour cream, eggs, and ½ cup of the bread crumbs; mix well and season with salt and pepper. Refrigerate, covered, for 2 hours or up to 1 day.

Remove the corn cake mixture from the refrigerator. Using about 1½ tablespoons at a time, form into 12 patties. Coat all sides with bread crumbs and refrigerate for 1 hour.

Heat ½ inch of vegetable oil in a very large, nonstick sauté pan over moderately high heat. When the oil is hot, add a batch of the cakes and cook until golden brown on the first side, about 1 minute. Carefully flip, using a rubber spatula, and cook the second side until golden brown. Drain on paper towels and serve immediately with sprigs of cilantro and Chipotle Mayonnaise.

Note: If your chipotle peppers are dried rather than canned, soak them for 2 to 3 hours in warm water to cover until soft and pliable, and stem, seed, and mince them before proceeding.

3 tablespoons olive oil

1 small bunch green onions, minced

½ cup chopped cilantro leaves

¾ cup sour cream

2 eggs, lightly beaten

1½ cups fine dried bread crumbs

Salt and pepper, to taste

Vegetable oil, for cooking

Cilantro sprigs, for garnish

Watermelon-Jicama Salad with Jalapeños

Jalapeño Syrup:

½ cup fresh lime juice

½ cup water

½ cup sugar

6 jalapeño peppers, stemmed and cut in thin rounds

2 cups seeded and cubed watermelon

1 small jicama, peeled and cut in julienne (1½ to 2 cups)

Mint sprigs, for garnish

This refreshing summer salad is simple and easy to prepare, and makes an outstanding appetizer or side dish to serve with grilled poultry or fish. Grilled prawns mixed into this combination would also be delicious.
Makes 4 servings.   Hotter: rated 6

To make the Jalapeño Syrup: Combine the lime juice, water, and sugar in a small saucepan. Bring to a boil over moderate heat. Boil for 10 to 15 minutes, until the mixture is thick and syrupy. Add the jalapeño pepper and cook for 5 minutes. Remove from the heat and cool to room temperature.

Arrange the watermelon and jicama on a plate. Drizzle the jalapeño syrup over the fruit, topping with the jalapeño rounds. Garnish with fresh mint, and serve slightly chilled or at cool room temperature.

Thai Squid Salad with Three Chilies

Dressing:

¼ cup peanut oil

2 tablespoons *nuoc cham* (fish sauce)

2 tablespoons fresh lime juice

Zest from 2 limes

3 cloves garlic, thinly sliced

2 jalapeño peppers or serrano chilies, cut in thin rounds

Salt and pepper, to taste

2 tablespooons peanut oil

3 cups cleaned squid bodies, cut into ½-inch rings, and tentacles (about 3 pounds whole squid bodies)

1 small red onion, halved and thinly sliced

1 red bell pepper, cut in julienne

3 jalapeño peppers, stemmed and cut in thin rounds

8 or more butter lettuce leaves

½ cup mint leaves

½ cup cilantro leaves

2 tablespoons dried red pepper flakes

½ cup roasted peanuts, coarsely chopped

This classic Thai salad is perfect for those on a low-fat, low-calorie diet. If squid is difficult to find, use small- or medium-sized prawns instead (remove shells and tails and cook in the peanut oil for 2 to 2½ minutes). This salad is at once hot and fiery, refreshing and invigorating.
Makes 4 to 6 servings.   *Hottest: rated 8*

To make the dressing: Place the peanut oil in a small bowl. Use a wire whisk to incorporate the fish sauce a little at a time, whisking all the while. Add the lime juice and the zest, garlic, and jalapeño peppers: mix well. Set aside at room temperature until needed.

Heat the oil in a large skillet over high heat. When the oil is hot, add the squid and cook, stirring constantly, for 1 to 1½ minutes or until the squid is just done. Do not overcook the squid or it will be tough and rubbery.

Place the squid in a large bowl along with the red onion, bell pepper, jalapeño pepper, and the dressing; mix well. Arrange on the lettuce leaves, and garnish with the mint, cilantro, red pepper flakes, and peanuts. Serve immediately.

Roasted Red Pepper Soup with Green Chilies and Smoked Chicken

1 large onion, coarsely chopped

3 cloves garlic, minced

3 tablespoons ground cayenne pepper or small red chilies

1½ tablespoons ground coriander

1 teaspoon each ground mace, cloves, and cumin

3 tablespoons olive oil

3 tablespoons unsalted butter

2 quarts light chicken stock

4 large roasted red bell peppers, peeled, seeded, and coarsely chopped

3 roasted California or other long green chilies, seeded, stemmed, and sliced into thin strips

1 cup cubed or shredded smoked chicken or turkey meat

Salt and pepper, to taste

½ cup créme fraîche, for garnish

Sweet, mild red bell peppers combined with fiery dried chilies form the base of this beautiful red soup. The smokey taste of both the roasted peppers and the chicken make for a flavorful and unusual cold-weather dish. If you prefer a milder soup, reduce the amount of cayenne or small red chilies to 1½ tablespoons. Serve warm tortillas or tortilla chips and a green salad alongside.
Makes 6 to 8 servings. *Hottest: rated 10*

In a large soup pot, cook the onion, garlic, and spices in the olive oil and butter over moderate heat for 10 minutes, stirring frequently. Add the chicken stock and red peppers and bring to a boil over high heat. Boil for 5 minutes, stirring frequently. Reduce the heat to moderate and cook for 15 minutes.

Cool the soup mixture to room temperature. Purée in a blender until smooth. Strain it through a fine wire mesh, and return it to the saucepan.

Bring the soup to a boil over high heat. Cook for 15 minutes over high heat, stirring frequently. Add all but a few strips of the roasted green chilies (chop the remaining chilies for garnish) and the chicken. Reduce heat to moderate and cook for 15 minutes. Season the soup with salt and pepper, and serve with a drizzle of crème fraîche and the chopped bits of the remaining green chilies.

Texas-Style Chili with Pinto Beans

1½ cups dry pinto beans, sorted

2 quarts water

Salt, to taste

4 each dried pasilla, ancho, and cascabel chilies

1 pound bacon

2 large onions, cut in small dice

6 cloves garlic, finely chopped

6 jalapeño peppers, finely chopped

2 pounds lean beef stew meat, finely chopped (not ground)

3 tablespoons chili powder

2 tablespoons each ground cumin, coriander, and cayenne

1 cup weak coffee

3 cups unsalted beef broth or stock

Salt and pepper, to taste

1 cup chopped cilantro or parsley, for garnish

As with most regional specialties, there are many versions of "authentic" Texas-style chili. Some cooks use beans while others insist that true chili consists of only meat, chilies, and seasonings. This version is deeply flavored, contains plump pinto beans, and uses a bit of coffee for a real cowboy flavor.
Makes 6 servings. *Hottest: rated 9*

Soak the beans in water for 12 hours or up to 1 day, changing the water every 8 hours. Drain and place in a saucepan with 2 quarts fresh water. Bring to a boil over high heat. Reduce the heat to moderately high and cook for 55 minutes to 1 hour or until the beans are tender but not mushy. Drain and season with salt. Set aside until needed.

Cover the chilies in boiling water and soak for 4 to 6 hours or until they are soft and pliable. Remove the seeds and stems and, using a bit of the soaking liquid, purée in a blender until smooth. Set aside until needed.

In a large saucepan, cook the bacon until crisp. Remove with a slotted spoon and drain on paper towels. Discard all but ¼ cup of the bacon fat. Coarsely chop the bacon and add to the beans.

Cook the onion, garlic, and jalapeño peppers in the remaining bacon fat over moderate heat for 10 minutes, stirring from time to time. Add the meat and spices and cook over high heat for 5 minutes, stirring constantly. Add the coffee, beef broth, and the reserved puréed chilies, and bring to a boil. Reduce the heat to moderately low, and cook for 1 hour to 1½ hours, stirring from time to time. When the meat is tender, add the beans and bacon; mix gently. Cook for 15 minutes, season with pepper and more salt if needed, and serve with a garnish of chopped cilantro or parsley.

Cheese-Stuffed Peppers with Ancho Chili Sauce

This dish is made with mild sweet peppers filled with ground meat, rice, or both in eastern Europe; with temperate peppers in the Mediterranean; and with fiery chili peppers in Central and South America. The quintessential hot chili recipe, this one is for dedicated hotheads.
Makes 4 to 6 servings.   *Hottest: rated 10*

To make the Ancho Chili Sauce: Soak the dried chilies in 2 cups of boiling water for 4 to 6 hours, or until they are soft and pliable. Drain, reserving the soaking liquid. Stem and seed the chilies and coarsely chop. Set aside the chilies and the soaking liquid separately (and the puréed chipotle pepper, if used) until needed.

In a large saucepan, cook the onion, garlic, spices, and oregano in the olive oil over moderate heat for 10 minutes, stirring from time to time. Add the chilies and 2 cups of soaking liquid and bring to a boil over high heat. Reduce the heat to moderately high and cook for 15 minutes. Remove from the heat and cool slightly.

Purée the sauce in a blender and strain through a fine wire mesh. Return it to the saucepan, season with salt and pepper, and keep warm until needed. (Or the sauce can be refrigerated for up to 1 week.)

Preheat oven to 375° F.

Roast the fresh chilies until the skins just turn black. When cool enough to handle, carefully remove the skins, taking care not to break or tear the flesh of the chilies. Starting from the stem end, make a 1-inch slit in each chili. Gently remove the seeds and the interior portion of the stem; discard.

Combine the cheeses and cumin seed in a bowl; mix well. Carefully fill each pepper with the cheese mixture, once again taking care not to tear the chilies. Place the filled chilies in a lightly greased shallow baking dish and bake for 12 to 15 minutes or until the cheese is melted.

Remove chilies from the oven and serve on pools of the Ancho Chili Sauce. Garnish with a drizzle of Mexican crema, crème fraîche, or sour cream and sprigs of fresh oregano or cilantro.

Ancho Chili Sauce:

3 dried ancho chilies, coarsely chopped

3 dried poblano chilies, coarsely chopped

2 chipotle peppers (or 2 tablespoons puréed chipotle pepper)

2 cups boiling water

1 small red onion, coarsely chopped

3 cloves garlic, minced

1 teaspoon each ground mace, cinnamon, and oregano

¼ cup olive oil

Salt and pepper, to taste

6 large fresh poblano or California green chilies

½ pound Monterey Jack cheese, grated

¼ pound smoked Mozzarella or other natural smoked cheese, grated

¼ pound Asiago (or other hard grating cheese), grated

1 tablespoon cumin seed

Mexican crema, crème fraîche, or sour cream, for garnish

African Fire Pork Stew

12 small dried red chilies

3 pounds pork butt, trimmed
of excess fat and tendon, cut in
1-inch pieces (about 3 cups
chopped pork meat)

2 large onions, cut in
large dice

6 cloves garlic, coarsely
chopped

6 jalapeño peppers, seeded,
stemmed, and coarsely
chopped

⅓ cup peanut oil

2-inch piece ginger root,
peeled and coarsely chopped

1 tablespoon paprika

2 teaspoons each ground
nutmeg, coriander, cinnamon,
and allspice

2 tablespoons dark brown sugar

5 cups unsalted beef broth
or stock

3 cups peeled and chopped
tomatoes, or a 28-ounce can
tomatoes

¾ cup roasted peanuts

4 medium sweet potatoes,
peeled and cut into ¾-inch
pieces

¼ cup red wine vinegar

If you are a true chili pepper enthusiast you will have to try this incendiary North African pork stew. In Africa, hot dishes are made even hotter with a sauce called berbere—a mixture of chilies, spices, and tomatoes. If you need extra heat in this stew, add a tablespoon of dried red pepper flakes or a dash of prepared hot sauce, but I would sample a few spoonfuls before adding any more chilies. Makes 6 servings. Hottest: rated 9

Cover the dried chilies in boiling water and soak for 2 to 3 hours or until they are soft. Drain and coarsely chop. Set aside until needed.

Cook the pork, onions, garlic, and jalapeño peppers in the peanut oil over high heat for 7 to 10 minutes, stirring all the while. Add the ginger, spices, and sugar and cook over moderate heat for 5 minutes, stirring frequently. Add the beef broth and bring to a boil over high heat. Add the tomatoes, peanuts, and reserved chilies, reduce the heat to moderate, and cook for 1 hour, stirring from time to time.

Add the potatoes and vinegar and cook for 25 to 30 minutes or until the meat and potatoes are tender. Season with salt and pepper and garnish with chopped parsley to taste.

Chicken Mole

Don't be scared away by the long list of ingredients—all but three are cooked together in one pot and then puréed. A good mole has layers of flavor and different intensities of heat, which come from many different chilies and long, slow cooking. It improves with age and is best the second or third day. Serve this poultry dish with rice and corn tortillas and sautéed zucchini or pattypan squash. Makes 10 to 12 servings. Hottest: rated 10

To make the mole: Place the chilies, tomatoes, onion, garlic, jalapeños, spices and herbs, and water in a heavy-bottomed, large saucepan. Bring to a boil over high heat. Cook for 10 minutes, stirring frequently. Reduce the heat to moderate, and simmer for 1 to 1½ hours, or until the mixture is slightly thick and aromatic. Cool to room temperature. Purée in a blender until smooth. Strain through a wire mesh and return to the saucepan.

Add the chocolate and peanut butter and bring the sauce to a boil. Reduce the heat to low and simmer for 30 minutes, stirring frequently. Season with salt and pepper. At this point the sauce can be stored, covered, in the refrigerator for up to 1 week.

Preheat oven to 400° F.

In a large nonstick skillet, brown the chicken on all sides in batches. Divide the chicken and mole between two large baking dishes, and cover with tin foil. Bake for 45 to 50 minutes, or until the chicken is tender and cooked all the way through. Drizzle with lime juice, garnish with chopped cilantro, and serve immediately.

Note: Alternately, use only 1 large chicken plus 2 extra legs. In this case, use only half of the sauce in one baking dish, and half of the lime juice and cilantro when serving. Freeze the remaining sauce in a tightly sealed container for up to 4 months, or refrigerate for 5 days.

Mole:

4 dried pasilla chilies

4 dried ancho chilies

3 dried small Asian or Italian red chilies

3 chipotle peppers

2 dried California or nuevo Mexicana chilies

4 jalapeño peppers, stemmed, seeded, and chopped

3 medium tomatoes, chopped

1 large onion, coarsely chopped

4 cloves garlic, chopped

1 tablespoon each ground cinnamon, cumin, coriander, and black pepper

2 teaspoons each ground mace, cloves, and oregano

3½ quarts water

3 ounces semisweet chocolate

⅓ cup smooth peanut butter

Salt and pepper, to taste

2 large chickens (4 to 4½ pounds each), plus four extra legs, cut into serving pieces (see Note)

Juice from 3 limes

1½ cups chopped cilantro, for garnish

Walnut-Fig Tart with Ancho Chilies

Dough:

2 cups all-purpose flour

½ cup sugar

1 teaspoon salt

½ pound (2 sticks) chilled
unsalted butter, cut into
24 chunks

3 to 5 tablespoons cold water

Filling:

5 dried pasilla or ancho chilies

2½ cups dried figs, stemmed
and coarsely chopped

2 cups white wine

¾ cup sugar

4 tablespoons (½ stick)
unsalted butter

¼ cup bourbon or whiskey

1 tablespoon vanilla extract

1 cup coarsely chopped
walnuts

Dash cayenne pepper

Créme fraîche or vanilla ice
cream (optional)

Blond dried calmyrna figs combined with dried ancho chilies makes an unusual filling for this handsome tart. The chilies blend with the sweet figs and walnuts, producing a finely balanced and unusual pastry. Serve with sherry for a unique dessert.
Makes 6 to 8 servings. Hot: rated 1

To make the dough: Place the flour, sugar, and salt in a bowl; mix well. Add the butter and, with your fingers, combine just until the mixture resembles coarse meal. Add the water and form into a ball. Wrap in plastic and refrigerate for 2 hours or up to 2 days.

Cover the chilies with boiling water to cover, and let soak for 2 to 3 hours or until they are soft and pliable. Remove the seeds and stems, finely chop, and set aside until needed.

Preheat oven to 375° F.

Remove the dough from the refrigerator ½ hour before you plan to bake it. Press the dough into a 10-inch tart pan; make an even bottom layer, press up the sides, and extend a ¼- to ½-inch ridge above the top edge of the tart pan. Cover with parchment paper or foil, fill with pie weights or dried beans, and bake for 20 minutes. Remove the paper and weights, re-cover only the edges, and bake for 10 to 15 minutes more or until the crust is just turning very light brown. Remove from the oven and let cool to room temperature before filling.

Meanwhile, to prepare the filling: Place the figs, wine, and sugar in a heavy-bottomed saucepan. Bring to a boil over high heat. Reduce the heat to moderate and cook for 10 to 15 minutes or until the figs are tender and the liquid is syrupy. Add the butter, bourbon, vanilla extract, walnuts, cayenne pepper, and reserved chilies; mix well until the butter is melted. Remove from the heat and cool.

Fill the tart shell and serve, optionally with a drizzle of crèm fraîche or vanilla ice cream.

Jalapeño-Lime Ice

3 cups water

2 cups sugar

8 jalapeño peppers, coarsely chopped

1¼ cups coarsely chopped mint leaves

½ cup fresh lime juice

4 cups ice cubes

Mint sprigs, for garnish

Lime slices, for garnish

Refreshing and stimulating, this sweet-hot concoction can be served for dessert, after a spicy meal, or between courses for an unusual palate cleanser and to restore the appetite. For a more pronounced mint flavor, mince 3 tablespoons of fresh mint leaves and stir them in just before serving.
Makes 6 servings. Hotter: rated 6

Place the water, sugar, jalapeño peppers, mint, and lime juice in a large, heavy-bottomed saucepan. Bring to a boil over high heat. Boil for 25 to 30 minutes, stirring frequently. Remove from the heat and cool slightly. Strain the liquid, and place in a covered nonreactive container in the freezer for 6 hours or up to 2 days. (The mixture won't freeze but will become slushy and icy.)

Using a cleaver or heavy object, slightly crush the ice cubes. Place ice cubes in a blender along with the jalapeño-lime mixture. Blend until the ice is finely crushed. Serve immediately, garnished with sprigs of fresh mint and lime slices.

Chocolate-Chili Cake with Mocha Frosting

3 large dried ancho chilies

3 chipotle peppers

½ cup water

½ pound (2 sticks) unsalted butter

4 ounces unsweetened chocolate

½ cup Dutch process cocoa

2 large eggs, at room temperature

2½ cups granulated sugar

1 cup buttermilk

1 tablespoon almond extract

2 cups all-purpose flour

1 teaspoon baking soda

1 tablespoon ground cinnamon

¼ teaspoon salt

Mocha Frosting:

8 ounces bittersweet chocolate

2 tablespoons water

½ pound (2 sticks) unsalted butter, softened

1 tablespoon very finely ground dark roast coffee

3 cups confectioner's sugar

1½ cups coarsely chopped toasted almonds, for garnish

This dessert combination of bittersweet chocolate and dusky dried chilies isn't so strange when you consider their happy pairing in Mexican mole sauce. This is a sort of reverse mole sauce—heavy on the sweet and chocolate, light on the spicy essence of chili peppers. If you have the same passions for chocolate and hot chilies that I do, you won't be disappointed by this exotic cake recipe.
Makes 8 to 10 servings.   Hot: rated 2

Preheat oven to 350° F.

Soak the chilies in water to cover overnight or until soft and pliable. Remove the seeds and stems and discard the water. Using a blender, purée the ancho chilies and the chipotle peppers in the ½ cup water until smooth.

Melt the butter and chocolate with the cocoa over low heat, stirring often until butter and chocolate are completely melted. Place the eggs, sugar, buttermilk, and almond extract in a large bowl; mix well. Add the dry ingredients (no need to sift) to the buttermilk mixture and mix well. Add the butter-chocolate mixture and the chilies; mix well.

Grease and flour 3 cake pans. Distribute the batter evenly among the pans. Bake for 25 to 30 minutes or until a toothpick inserted in the center comes out clean. Let cakes cool before removing from the pans.

To make the Mocha Frosting: Melt the chocolate and the water over very low heat until the chocolate is melted, stir to combine, and cool to room temperature. Combine the chocolate, butter, and coffee in a bowl. Add the sugar and beat at high speed with an electric mixer until the mixture is smooth and creamy.

Assemble the cake by placing one layer on a large plate. Frost the top, cover with second layer, frost the top of it, and top with last layer. Frost the top of the cake and the sides. Garnish the edges with the almonds.

INDEX

Index of Recipes

Index

Sue White and Joyce Oudkerk Pool
would like to thank the following people.

Sandra Griswald . . . . *props*

Ina Glickstein . . . . *food styling assisting*

Elizabeth Fall . . . . *photo assisting*

Dan Bowe . . . . *props*

Eric Powell . . . . *backgrounds*

F. Dorian on 388 Hayes St. . . . . *props*

Gibson Scheid . . . . *on-going support*